Ia

A Wholly H
American Bagpipe   omedies

A Wholly Healthy Glasgow: 'The funniest play I have seen for months' *The Times*

American Bagpipes: 'A first-class piece of sharp-fanged comedy that means business!' *Guardian*

The Sex Comedies: 'A funny and hugely enjoyable experience, all the more so because there is always a sense of frustration, emptiness and desperation.' *What's On*

Iain Heggie's first play, *A Wholly Healthy Glasgow* (1985), won the Special Prize in the inaugural Mobil Playwriting Competition and was subsequently produced by the Royal Exchange Theatre, Manchester, where he was Arts Council writer in residence, before transferring to the Royal Court Theatre, London, in 1988. Other work includes *American Bagpipes* (Royal Exchange, 1988, and Royal Court, 1989); *Clyde Nouveau* (Edinburgh Festival, 1989); *The Sex Comedies* (1992); *Tourist Variations*, a libretto (Edinburgh Festival, 1993); two one-act plays, *Lust* and *Politics in the Park* (1986); and *An Experienced Woman Gives Advice* (Royal Exchange, 1995). Both *King of Scotland* (2000) and *Wiping My Mother's Arse* (Traverse Theatre, 2001) won Scotsman Fringe Firsts. He won the John Whiting Award in 1988. Iain Heggie also teaches acting and improvisation at the Royal Scottish Academy of Music and Drama. He made his directorial debut with Martin McDonagh's *The Beauty Queen of Leenane* (Tron Theatre, 2001) and has also directed *The Don* (RSAMD, 2002).

by the same author and available from Methuen

An Experienced Woman Gives Advice
Wiping My Mother's Arse
Love Freaks

IAIN HEGGIE

Plays: 1

A Wholly Healthy Glasgow

American Bagpipes

The Sex Comedies

introduced by the author

Methuen Drama

METHUEN CONTEMPORARY DRAMATISTS

1 3 5 7 9 10 8 6 4 2

This collection first published in Great Britain in 2003 by
Methuen Publishing Limited,
215 Vauxhall Bridge Road, London SW1V 1EJ

A Wholly Healthy Glasgow was first published by Methuen London Ltd in 1988
Copyright © Iain Heggie 1988, 2003
American Bagpipes was first published by Penguin Books in 1989
Copyright © Iain Heggie 1989, 2003
Introduction copyright © 2003 by Iain Heggie

Iain Heggie has asserted his right under the Copyright, Designs and Patents
Act, 1988, to be identified as the author of this work

Methuen Publishing Limited Reg. No. 3543167

A CIP catalogue record for this book is available from the British Library.

ISBN 0 413 77206 3

Typeset in Baskerville by MATS, Southend-on-Sea, Essex
Printed and bound in Great Britain by
Cox & Wyman Ltd, Reading, Berkshire

Caution

Contents

Iain Heggie:
A Chronology

1986 *Politics in the Park* opened at the Liverpool Playhouse. It has since been presented in many fringe and amateur productions and was produced in Toronto in 1993.

1987 *A Wholly Healthy Glasgow* opened at the Royal Exchange Theatre, Manchester, then at the Edinburgh Festival and the Royal Court Theatre, London, in 1988. It toured Scotland in 1993. It won the Special Prize in the inaugural Mobil Playwriting Competition in 1985. Iain Heggie was Arts Council writer-in-residence at the Royal Exchange Theatre, Manchester.

1988 *American Bagpipes* opened at the Royal Exchange Theatre, Manchester, in 1988 and the Royal Court Theatre, London, in 1989. It won the 1988 John Whiting Award and the *Manchester Evening News* Best New Play award. In 1989 it opened at the Soho Rep in New York. It was also performed in Finland and in Canada.

1989 *Clyde Nouveau* opened at the Edinburgh International Festival at the Churchill Theatre.

1992 *Lust,* a monologue, opened at the Gilded Balloon, Edinburgh, and transferred to the Arches in Glasgow. It was a finalist in the London One-Man Play Festival in 1994.

      The Sex Comedies opened at the Traverse in 1992 and transferred to the CCA in Glasgow before opening at the Old Red Lion in 1993. It has also toured Germany and Austria.

1993 *Tourist Variations,* libretto of an opera by James Macmillan, opened at the Edinburgh International Festival at the Traverse Theatre.

1995 *An Experienced Woman Gives Advice* opened at the Royal Exchange Theatre in Manchester. It was nominated for the *Manchester Evening News* Best Play Award in 1996 and was produced at the Royal Lyceum Theatre, in Edinburgh, in 1998. It has been translated into Italian.

The Pen shown in cinemas and on the BBC as part of the Tartan Shorts scheme.

1997 *Lavochkin-5*, a translation of the Russian play by Alexei Shipenko, opened at the Tron Theatre in Glasgow.

1998 *Don Juan*, an adaptation of Molière's play, toured Britain and Ireland for Theatre Basel.

2000 *King of Scotland* opened at the Assembly Rooms, Edinburgh, and won a *Scotsman* Fringe First.

Funeral Catering in the Twenty-first Century was performed on Radio 4.

The Actor's Agent's Tale was broadcast as part of 2,000 tales on Radios 3 and 4.

2001 *Wiping My Mother's Arse* opened at the Traverse Theatre, Edinburgh, and won a *Scotman* Fringe First. It has been translated in four languages and is being produced in Australia and the USA in 2003.

2002 *Love Freaks*, an adaptation of Marivaux's *Double Inconstancy*, opened at the Tron Theatre, Glasgow.

The Don opened at the Royal Scottish Academy of Music and Drama

The Zeitgeist Man was broadcast on Radio 4.

Introduction

Having never consciously set out to be controversial I was gobsmacked when the second public performance of *A Wholly Healthy Glasgow* in Manchester saw two hundred people leave before the interval. Because the Royal Exchange is a theatre in the round most of the departures were conspicuous, even when they weren't accompanied by noisy expressions of disgust. I didn't realise at the time but this experience soon taught me that it was one of the first British plays to saturate the audience in obscene language. Being my first full-length play, it was, I suppose, what journalists like to call a baptism by fire. The play got me a reputation for being an angry writer. This, I take it, is a response to the language, as to me the *action* of the play is probably the lightest of anything I've written. I see subsequent plays such as *An Experienced Woman Gives Advice*, *Wiping My Mother's Arse*, *King of Scotland* and *The Don* as much more aggressive comedies. *A Wholly Healthy Glasgow* was too long in its original version. Subsequent productions and this republication have given me the opportunity to cut more than twenty minutes from its running time.

American Bagpipes is my most performed play. I'm sure this is due in no small measure to the brilliance of the original production by the late great Caspar Wrede. He insisted that my work had a closer relationship to the pre-twentieth-century high comedies than to the more naturalistic comedies of our time. Whether he was right or not he certainly incited the most courageous and disciplined performance I've ever seen of my work. The fault with the original version of the play was that it was overcomplicated, understructured and its ambitions were in excess of my ability, at that time, to bring it all together. This new version is more solidly constructed, simpler and a wee bit lighter.

As an acting teacher I have spent a large amount of my life

watching actors improvise short situations. This has inspired me to write short plays. In 1992 I grouped some of them together as *The Sex Comedies*. They are included unchanged from the original.

Iain Heggie
Glasgow, 2002

A Wholly Healthy Glasgow

A Wholly Healthy Glasgow was first performed at the Royal Exchange Theatre, Manchester, on 29 January 1987. It was revived for the Edinburgh Festival 1987 and then played at the Royal Court Theatre, London, in 1988. The cast was as follows:

Donald Dick	Tom Watson
Charley Hood	Gerard Kelly
Murdo Caldwell	Paul Higgins

Directed by Richard Wilson
Designed by Sue Plummer

Characters

Donald Dick
Charley Hood
Murdo Caldwell

Setting

The massage room of the Spartan Health Club, Glasgow.

Note on layout

The mark / indicates an interruption:

1) when a character breaks his own train of thought:

> **Charley**   . . . And. You *couldn't* line yourself a line up.
> Because let's face it about you Donny, you are nothing
> but a/ lined *your own* line up? Because for *Fuck's* sake . . .
> etc.

2) when one character is interrupted by another where:

> a) the character returns to his own train of thought after
>   the other one has finished:
>
> **Donald**   I didn't say it:/
> **Charley**   Because you say I've just gone and/
> **Donald**   I didn't say it:/
> **Charley**   You say I've just gone and that leaves me . . .
> etc.

> b) the character changes his emphasis or train of thought
>   after the other has finished:
>
> **Charley**   I think that's the/
> **Donald**   That has to be the/
> **Charley**   Oh mammy, daddy, it can't be the/
> **Donald/Charley**   It's the new instructor.

Act One

As the lights come up, **Donald** *comes in from reception. He carries a small closed circuit monitor. He plugs it in and experiments with locations before settling down to watch it from a swivel chair.*

Charley *comes in from reception.*

Charley   So Donny boy, son. See me.

Donald   Heh Charley: see you.

Charley   Today I am some kind of good guy.

Donald   Divert the shite elsewhere, uh? I'm/

Charley   Today I/

Donald   I'm occupied.

Charley *takes out and lights cigarette, unseen by* **Donald**.

So Donny boy, son.

Donald   All I'm wanting's/

Charley   So *don't* look at us.

Donald   All I'm wanting's *decapitation plans for the new boy.*

Charley   So the day's all going *my* way.

Donald   Plans for/

Charley   All *our* way.

Donald   Plans for *the new instructor.*

Donald *turns sharply to* **Charley**. **Charley** *conceals cigarette.*

Charley   So there's time the morrow for the new boy.

Donald   Aye but/

Charley   And don't hatchet my happiness.

Donald   Aye but/

Charley   Because *don't remind me* about the new boy.

Donald   Bobby phoned up!

Charley *takes a puff.*

Charley   Did that prick and a half Bobby want?

Donald   So plans the night, right.

Charley   And. I will bend the earholes to your heavy jobbying breath about the new boy, *the morrow.*

Donald   *The night.*

Charley   Ach aye: the night. (If there's time.)

Donald   There's *going to be* time. (Four jobbying hours till we shut.)

Charley   *As long* as there's time.

Donald   There's time *definitely.* (The new boy starts *the morrow.*)

Charley   A guy's to get time to *operate.* (The morrow?)

Donald   The morrow.

Charley   *Does the new boy fuck* start the morrow. Starts *Tuesday.*

Donald   Bobby *phoned up!*

Charley *takes a puff.*

Charley   So fuck's the new boy starting the morrow for?

Donald   So plans the night.

Charley   The new boys *always* start Tuesday.

Donald   Because we/

Charley   And. The morrow's Monday.

Donald   We have got to plan.

Charley   The new boys *always* get their first day *off.*

Donald   Plan to *get rid* of the new boy.

Charley   They always get *the Monday* off.

Donald   A bastarding, *interfering* new boy.

Charley   The Monday off after the ten day two weekend initiation training course at Pontefract.

Donald   So plans the night, right?

Charley   Pontefract jobbying head office.

Donald   Because no plans to get rid of the new instructor and/ and/ . . . (I'm occupied.)

Donald *adjusts closed circuit.*

Charley   What's this new boy's name?

Donald   I don't know.

Charley   Didn't you ask.

Donald   No.

Charley   Didn't Bobby say?

Donald   Did he fuck . . . Because I don't care.

Charley   Neither do I. (Fuck.) But you kill me. So ra ha ha. Aye ra ha ha and today's been kind of *ecstatic* this far. And. There's a fly man waiting for me at the bar, the Empire Hotel with a fur coat. (Ta ra.)

Donald   A fur coat's fuck all use *to me*.

Charley   The fur coat's *not for you*.

Donald   So don't tell us about the bastard.

Charley   It's for Alana.

Alana (*off, on tannoy*)   If Mr McGuigan is in the gym, would he come to reception, please? We have a telephone call for you.

Charley   Aye ra ha ha, Donny. So let me just *listen* to my Alana. *Listen?* Let me just *look* at my Alana.

He goes to closed circuit screen.

So switch up to reception.

Donald   Och/

Charley *forcibly adjusts closed circuit.*

Alana (*off, on tannoy*)   If Mr McGuigan is in the gym, would he come to reception, please? We have a telephone call for you.

Charley   So. That's my Alana. And she sits up at reception. Aye, that's my Alana and take over from her, uh, Donny?

Donald   Och I'm all right here.

Charley   Do us a favour, the once.

Donald   I'm all right *as I am.*

Donald *adjusts closed circuit.*

Charley   So come on to fuck, Donny. The fly man might take a walk I'm not back to him before six. And. Because: the Alana's to *try the fur coat on* at the bar, the Empire Hotel.

Donald   So you take her about, she tries stuff on, you pay?

Charley   Oh ho now Donny: the Alana!

Donald   You big soft cunt you.

Charley   She goes about with me, she tries stuff on, *nobody* pays. Because the Alana, me are 'the gruesome bastarding twosome'. (Ta ra.)

Charley *takes a puff.*

I mean Donny: I would hardly go about with her if she was a prick. (Consult your nut, uh?) *She* aye *she* gets to swagger round ten minutes in half a leopard, say 'Piss off shiteface, I'm not buying it' to the flyman, she's happy. So Donny boy: do the favour, uh? (I'm laughing for you.)

Charley *goes to take a puff.*

Donald *slowly turns to look at* **Charley**. **Charley** *hides his* *cigarette.* **Donald** *turns away again.* **Charley** *goes to take a puff.*

Donald   Get that fag out.

Charley *chokes.*

Donald   Because what have I told you about smoking in my massage chambers?

Charley *chokes louder.*

Donald   I got my atmosphere to think about.

Charley *chokes louder, loses cigarette.*

Donald   And when my good shagpile comes back down here no more cigarette ends are getting stubbed out in it, OK?

Charley *finds cigarette and stubs it out.*

Donald *turns away and stares at closed circuit.*

Charley   What are you looking at?

Donald   None of your business.

Charley   Because what *are* you looking at?

Donald   Never you mind.

Charley   Because whatever you're looking at/

He spins **Donald**'s *chair.*

You can't see it now.

Donald   Bastard you . . . I'll/ I'll/ I'll

Chair stops spinning.

I'm occupied.

Donald *adjusts closed circuit.*

Charley   So time to acquaint ourselves the bastarding *business* aspect, eh? Now Donny: Last day the month's the day. And. Club's £100 short the break even *for* the month. And. Meaning. *I'm* £100 short my bonus. And. We get by the break even it stops Bobby coming from Pontefract to see *why* we're

not getting by the break even. (I say to Bobby: 'No chance
breaking even August, Bobby. Glasgow's evacuated Tenerife.
Glasgow's shagging tit the beach Corfu. Glasgow's chucking
up paella the pavement Majorca. He listen? He fuck.) Now. As
it happens, Donny, I've got this punter on. Due in. Any
minute. A beauty. A cinch. A *renewal*. So sit up reception
Donny, hold on to the giant shite for me he walks in the door.
Meanwhile I'll ensure Alana doesn't exceed a quick swagger
up down the bar, the Empire Hotel, the fur coat. Then. Nip
back here, pin down the renewal boy, knock the cash up by
the break even, collect my bonus. So take over reception the
Alana, uh?

Donald   Away to buggery.

Charley   But my bonus, Donny. *You know* my bonus pays
my lifestyle. Heh: the *minimum requirement* my lifestyle. Namely:
me Alana. Tanked up. Champagne cocktails. Nightly.

Donald   How come you want the Alana off reception?

Charley   I/ The fur coat, *I says*.

Donald   Fur coat be fucked. Because *you* can take over
reception, the Alana.

Charley   Aye and *oh* no.

Donald   The Alana'll be making it to the bar, the Empire
Hotel *on her own*.

Charley   Oh no *definitely*.

Donald   Because Bobby phoned up.

Charley   So?

Donald   And Bobby's phoning back.

Charley   Oh? . . . And?

Donald   He's phoning *you* back.

Charley   Me?

Donald   In *five* minutes.

Charley   What's he phoning me/? (Five?) I says to you:
Always inform the prick I've *just* gone.

Donald   I always do say: 'He's *just* gone, My Bybugger.'
(Normally.)

Charley   So *keep* saying it.

Donald   Why should I? (Fuck.)

Charley   Why *didn't* you say it?

Donald   I didn't say it:/

Charley   Because you say I've just gone and/

Donald   I didn't say it:/

Charley   You say I've just gone and that leaves me thirty
minutes from the time he phones up.

Donald   I didn't say it/ the deplorable *bastarding abuse* I've to
take from you. I mean: you've been out, you've been in all
fucking day. You've been out, you've been in, instead of
standing up the front door grabbing punters off the street to
line me up. Pricks like you lack dignity. I'm occupied.

Donald *adjusts set.*

Charley   So what *are* you looking at?

Donald   Never you mind.

Charley   I/ You're looking out for punters the massage.

Donald   Not at all.

Charley   You enterprising geriatric fuck. *I* line you up your
punters the massage.

Donald   When was the last time?

Charley   It's August.

Donald   Ignorant cunt.

Charley   August, I says.

Donald   Yes, *when was* the last time you lined me up a punter the massage?/A punter the massage lay/

Charley   It's August. (Fuck.) There's no punters out the street for me to line you up? (What?)

Donald   A punter the massage *lay down converted to the après-massage?*

Charley   I/

He takes out, lights a cigarette.

So Bobby's Pontefract head office?

Donald   I don't know. I/

Charley   You not hear a scabby Yorkshire accent the background?

Donald   No.

Charley *takes a puff.*

Charley   But how *could* you say Bobby I'd be back five minutes? What if I'm out more five minutes, uh? Because you're not here you say you're going be here Bobby comes from Pontefract.

Donald   Bobby comes from Pontefract will make fuck all difference to me.

Charley   Bobby comes from Pontefract he won't turn the blind eye to the après-massage.

Donald   Fuck all difference. (By the way.) I don't get any après-massage. (Do I?)

Pause.

Charley   So you definitely told Bobby I'd be back five minutes?

Donald   Definitely Charley, so I did.

Charley   Jesus fucking God Donny that's me *stuck here.*

He takes a puff.

So Donny: *you'll* have to take Alana the bar, the Empire Hotel.

Donald   Och away chase your jobby round a U-bend, Charley. I'm occupied.

He adjusts closed circuit.

And get that cigarette out. (I've got my shagpile to think about.)

Charley *goes to take another puff, but interrupts himself.*

Charley   Your *shagpile*? I wish you'd take your shagpile and – Heh wait a minute. Where *is* your shagpile?

Donald   Upstairs.

Charley   Because is that you *hiding* your shagpile?

Donald   It's drying out upstairs, *I said.*

Charley   Your fucking stupid-looking shagpile.

Donald   That shagpile was given to me by an admirer.

Charley   I/

Charley *takes a puff.*

Donald   And get that cigarette *out*, I says . . . Because you've been out, you've been in all jobbying day. Instead of helping me wash and handpick forty-eight cigarette ends *out* my shagpile.

Donald *produces and gives to* **Charley** *a goldfish bowl crammed with cigarette ends.* **Charley** *flicks ash into it and gives it back.*

Charley   So see this renewal punter of mine, Donny, guess what he does for a living?

Donald   Who cares?

Charley   Guess his career.

Donald   No.

Charley   I have often heard you remark the career can add the dash of spice to the après-massage.

Donald   I/

Charley   Because see this punter's career, Donny. This punter's career is: *professional jobbing footballer*. (Ta ra.)

He takes a puff.

And. The name of my punter *is* Craigie Stein. *Oh* aye. Craigie Stein, the big time international footballer. (Ta ra.)

Charley *takes a blatant puff, puts cigarette out into goldfish bowl and puts it down.*

Donald   Don't kid.

Charley   Craigie Stein *himself*!

Donald   International footballers don't sign up at back-alley health joints.

Charley   I thought this *myself* until the cunt staggered in here Thursday night *steaming drunk* and a battered-in kneecap. Because Craigie Stein's the mental bampot had his kneecap kicked fuck out of a year ago. And. His kneecap has not recuperated. And. So his club has given the boy the boot. And. Therefore I stepped right up to Craigie Stein sold him the buy-now-cheap-rate-new-enrolment special at £200 for the year. Oh aye: I sold the poor bastard *his hope*. And. He'll be in again any minute I'm hitting him a buy-now-cheap-rate-early-*renewal* special at £150 for the *second* year. (Taking me *right by* the break even.) . . . So you *taking* the Alana the bar, the Empire Hotel for us? . . . (I'll *definitely* line you up the Craigie Stein.) . . . Because engage the doll with alcohol a half an hour, uh? I'll pick her up later.

Charley *takes out cigarette packet. Discovers it is empty. Throws it away.*

Donald   How come you want the Alana off reception?

Charley   The fur coat, *I says*.

Donald   So I take her the bar, the Empire Hotel and she tries on the fur coats?

Charley   No.

Donald   No?

Charley   I mean: *no*! Because the fur coats are not important. I mean: I'll see to the fur coats later, OK?

Pause.

Donald   So why *do* you want the Alana off reception?

Charley   Why/? What is this? The fur/ Can we talk about this later? . . . Because come on to fuck the Craigie'll *be* here.

Donald   *Why?*

Charley   Because the Craigie's *due.*

Donald   *Why?*

Charley   Because . . . Because . . . Because the fur-coat story was a pack of brilliant lies, I thought up. (Ta ra.) . . . But it fooled you, uh?

Donald   Did it fuck.

Charley   It fooled you however?

Donald   I knew it was jobby from the kick off.

Charley   Is that right? So ra ha ha. Aye ra ha ha, Donny. So the Alana sees the footballer she turns the head. Because see the Alana, right? Alana goes for any guy gets his name the paper going. So say the Alana's sitting my taxi one night. I'm paying for it, back to *my* place. We're well bevvied up, I paid for it, not that I mind. I stop the taxi at one point, I pick up a paper. She reads it, I paid for it, not that I mind *definitely*. So the Alana sees a guy out the street. A guy out the street she says got his name the paper: the paper *she's reading*. So the Alana stops the taxi, gets out, *picks the other guy up.* (Some bird her, uh?) Meanwhile I'm left sitting our taxi, paying our taxi, paying *her share* our taxi, not that I mind. And. So I look the paper, I see this other guy, the guy the street, the guy got his name the paper, got his name the paper for flashing his dick. (Fuck.)

Pause.

Donald   Why can't you get casual about tit?

Charley   Because why can't you get casual about cock?

Pause.

Donald   So this Craigie's on for me?

Charley   On for you, Donny, no bother. I'll say to him: 'So this Donald – the touch – Dick: his hands the very ones get your career back on the rails,' I'll say to him. Wanting him, Donny?

Donald   Wanting him, Charley: The gorgeous bastard's got shoulders wide as a corporation bus. And because I need my nooky daily.

Charley   Nooky daily, Donny? Why's that?

Donald (*suddenly outraged*)   Because I am not an ornament on a mantelpiece, am I? . . . And plans to get rid the new boy the night?

Charley   Plans the night?

Donald   *The night.*

Charley   Because come on to/ Oh aye. The night. (Fuck.) The night, *definitely.*

Donald *turns back to closed circuit.*

Donald   Because the new boy's a keen cunt. (Apparently.)

Charley   So you take the Alana out the road and I definitely hold the Craigie for you. (Keen?)

Donald   Keen, so Bobby says.

Charley   Keen *will* be right. Aye, keen to cream off my best sales, my best *renewal* prospects maybe.

Donald   Bobby says the new boy *volunteered* to start a day early. (The morrow.) Haw heh: who's the dick down the gym?

Charley   So *take* the Alana, uh? (What?)

He looks at the screen.

No cunt I know.

Donald   And the body of a stallion too.

Charley   So *go*!

Donald   He's limped off the screen.

Charley   Go! (Limped?) Take a/

Donald   It's the footballer.

Charley   Take a shite. The footballer's not due *yet*. Switch over the changing rooms.

Donald *adjusts closed circuit.*

Charley   No. Up reception.

Donald *adjusts it again.*

Charley   No. Down the gym.

Donald *adjusts it again.*

Donald   Maybe the footballer came early.

Charley   I *don't let* my punters come early.

Donald   He was *drunk* Thursday, you talked to him. He was drunk, so he fails to understand: 'Don't for *fuck's* sake, come early.

Charley   So Donny:/

Donald   What, Charley?

Charley   The tool came early.

Pause.

Donald   So who's the object with him?

Charley   Heh: who's that measuring the leg?

Donald   The *inside* leg.

Charley   I think that the/

Donald   That has to be the/

Charley   Oh mammy, daddy, it can't be the/

Donald/Charley   It's the new instructor.

Pause.

Charley   And. Tuesday he/

Donald   Monday.

Charley   Tuesday *he* starts. (What?)

Donald   *Bobby said* Monday.

Charley   But this *isn't* Monday.

Donald   It's Sunday night, by fuck. And Bobby *said* this new boy is *keen*.

Charley   This isn't Monday/ (Keen? Aye: keen with my punter.)

Donald   *My* line up.

Charley   *Your* line up . . . so I'm *separating* the cunts.

Charley *goes to go.*

Donald   You're *not* separating them.

Charley   Get to fuck. *Of course* I'm separating them.

Donald   You separate them, the new boy gets ugly. In front of our punter.

Charley   (The using bastard!)

Pause.

Donald   Go reception, Charley, get the new boy up *the tannoy*. Bobby always gets the new boys to follow the tannoy.

Charley   OK. (Fuck.)

Donald   And look at *the way* the new boy's measuring him up.

Charley   And I've *already* measured him up.

Donald   To re-measure a punter had got to be despicable . . .

So did you mark his measurements on his card, for all to see?

Charley   Thursday night. The night he joined. Chest and waist.

Donald   So how come the new boy's measuring him up *again*?

Charley   And. If I see an early-cheap-rate-renewal contract coming out down there I'm/

Donald   So go, Charley.

Charley *is about to go. Telephone rings.* **Donald** *picks it up, listens in and quickly passes it to* **Charley**.

Donald   *I'll* go reception.

Charley (*to phone*)   Spartan Health. May we help you?

Donald *goes to go.*

Charley   Well hello, Mr Bybugger.

Donald *goes out to reception.*

Charley   Yes, Mr Bybugger.

Pause.

No, Mr Bybugger.

Donald (*off, on tannoy*)   Instructor to the massage chambers. Instructor to the massage chambers. Thanking you.

Charley   Yes, Mr Bybugger . . . grand, fine.

Donald   Would the instructor in the gym proceed to the massage chambers?

Charley   Oh yes, grand, fine.

Pause.

And what's the new instructor's name by the way, Mr Bybugger?

Donald   The *new* instructor to the massage chambers, please. *Now*, please. Thanking you.

Charley   Murdo . . . Murdo Caldwell, Mr Bybugger? . . .
Fine, grand, Mr Bybugger.

Donald   Would the new instructor *kindly* leave what he is
doing and go to the massage chambers?

Charley   No, no. The early arrival of a new instructor *suits us
fine*, Mr Bybugger. Yes, Mr Bybugger, certainly. Thanking you.

He puts phone down. He looks at closed circuit.

Unbelievable ignorant cunt.

Donald *comes in from reception, in haste.*

Donald   Unbelievable bent basket.

Charley   And./

Donald   Heh:/

Charley   So he *ignores* the calls.

Donald   Heh Charley:/

Charley   While he gives the bampot in the gym the
measuring tape treatment.

Donald   She's not there, Charley.

Charley   Imagine ignoring the calls. (What?) Cunts like that
have *definitely* lost the place. Because/ (What?)

Donald   The Alana's went.

Charley   Lost the bastarding place. She's not *went* (fuck),
she's/

Donald   She's went.

Charley   She's went? Haw heh: 'went' went home or 'went'
went to the lavvy?

Donald   She's *went*!

Pause. **Charley** *goes to closed circuit and checks.*

Charley   So. Donny: the new instructor's getting booted *the*
night.

Donald   Plans the night, booted the morrow.

Charley   Booted the night now, it'll have to be. Because Bobby phoned up. And. He's coming the morrow. And. We are not being seen slicing a hammer through the new boy's nut in front of Bobby. (Fuck.)

Charley *goes to go and thinks better of it.*

Charley   So I send Murdo up here, keep him quiet ten minutes, uh?

Donald   OK.

Charley   So put it there, uh?

He puts hand out, at a distance.

Donald   No.

Charley   How come?

Donald   I'm not putting it nowhere. If anyone's putting it anywhere, *you're* putting it *here*.

Charley *goes over to* **Donald** *and puts out hand to shake.* **Donald** *puts his out. At last second* **Charley** *diverts his hand and spins chair.*

Donald   Bastard you . . . You bastard . . . I'll/ I'll/ I'll/

Chair stops. **Charley** *goes to exit.*

Donald   Oh and Alana.

Charley   What about her?

Donald   She left a note. She'll phone you at some point.

Charley   . . . So the Alana phones in and I am with the renewal punter, enquire as to the bastarding *location*, the bastarding Alana, uh?

Charley *goes out to gym.*

Phone rings. **Donald** *answers.*

Donald   Spartan Health. May we help you?

He's just walked out Alana . . .

With a client, Alana . . .

Murdo *comes in from the gym.* **Murdo** *sees* **Donald***, he gestures apology and he goes to go.*

Donald (*to* **Murdo**)   Stay.
(*To phone.*) Someone here Alan, OK?
(*To* **Murdo**.) OK?
(*To phone.*) Aye. A nice night to you.

Donald *replaces the phone.*

Murdo   Do you work here?

Donald   I do. Heh:/

Murdo   Well I don't think he was right. (Sorry).

Donald   Hey you:/ (What?)

Murdo   An instructor came right up and *interrupted* me.

Donald   Well for a/

Murdo   When I was *halfway* through a company procedure.

Donald   For a start you're/

Murdo   Then he sent me up here.

Donald   You're/

Murdo   Could I have done something wrong?

Donald   You're/

Murdo   But I was halfway through the company procedure for *newly-enrolled members*. (Pardon?)

Donald   You're not supposed to be here yet.

Murdo (Sorry.)   Oh ah Mr Bybugger *said* I could come early.

Donald   He told *us* early meant tomorrow.

Murdo   Oh ah should I go home?

Donald   And. (What?) No!

Murdo   I *could* go home, if I *had* to.

Donald   You're going nowhere.

Murdo   I *wouldn't mind* if it's *wrong* of me to be here. (What, sorry?)

Donald   You *don't* leave a place, you're just arrived . . . Do you?

Murdo   Oh ah no. I mean; thanks. Because I *don't want* to go home. (So when I arrived from Pontefract I came straight here.)

Donald   The front of my door says 'Private'.

Murdo   Oh ah the other instructor told me to come in and wait.

Donald   We knock doors here.

Murdo   Because Mr Bybugger didn't mention knocking doors.

Donald   And how come you didn't answer the tannoy calls?

Murdo   Oh ah I couldn't. I/ Because Mr Bybugger says a new member's first visit *takes priority* over a tannoy/ I can smell cigarette smoke.

Donald   I doubt it.

Murdo   I'm sure I can smell cigarette smoke.

Donald   Because *no one* smokes in here. How come you didn't want to go home?

Murdo   Oh ah I can't/ I mean I prefer not to discuss it if that's/ (Sorry.) But it was also my enthusiasm which made me come early. (I have been told I've got a *lot* of enthusiasm.) . . . Where would the other instructor have gone to with the new member?

Donald   The fuck should I know.

Murdo   Because the instructor escorted the member *right out of the gym*.

Donald   Renewing the cunt's membership?

Murdo   Even though he was only *halfway through* his first visit. (Pardon?)

Donald   He'll be flogging the bastard an early-cheap-rate renewal.

Murdo   Oh ah but doesn't he know that Mr Bybugger says you can't offer an early-cheap-rate renewal until the *sixth* visit?

Donald   I know fuck all about it.

Murdo   By which time the member has had results and is able *to see* the advantages of the early-cheap-rate renewal. (What?)

Donald   I says: fuck all do I know about it.

Murdo   Oh ah *why?*

Donald   Because I *don't do* any renewals.

Murdo   Why don't you do any renewals?

Donald   Because I am not a greedy, money-grabbing bastard.

Pause.

Murdo   I'm sure I can smell cigarette smoke.

Donald   No.

Murdo   It smells *very like* cigarette smoke.

Donald   Because I don't permit smoking in my massage chambers. You were *thorough* the way you measured up that member.

Murdo   Oh ah. How did you see me? (Sorry) I mean: can I ask?

Donald *points to closed circuit.*

Donald   *Too* thorough.

Murdo   Oh ah Mr Bybugger says the closed circuit monitor is to be kept at reception and used for security checks only.

Donald   OK. So Charley Hood me, are doing a routine security check. So we saw you on the screen. We took one look at you and we knew we didn't know *who the hell you were*.

Murdo   If you didn't know it was me why did you say 'New instructor to reception' on the tannoy? (Sorry.)

Donald   We're brilliant guessers.

Pause.

Murdo   Well I didn't know you didn't know/ I'm not blaming *you*. You obviously *didn't know* I got permission to go to the gym.

Donald   *Permission?* Permission who from?

Murdo   The receptionist.

Donald   The receptionist?

Murdo   The girl.

Donald   Alana? Because 'the receptionist' and fuck off. You see the man in charge, you see *Charley Hood* before you act.

Murdo   I got permission.

Donald   Bobby would not like to know he has employed a total tit. (Permission from the receptionist!)

Murdo   Well sorry if I offended you.

Donald   What?

Murdo   Sorry if I offended you by not knocking your door.

Donald   Offended me?

Murdo   Or if I offended you by choosing not to discuss my family background.

Donald   Offended *me*?

Murdo   Or if I offended you by asking if you worked here.

Donald   I don't take offence.

Murdo   When I first arrived here/ Pardon?

Donald   The life I've had. It's made a brass-necked basket out of me. *I've* had *six* ambulances in *one week*, in my time. (Offended?)

Murdo   Well when I first arrived I did ask you if you worked here.

Donald   Aye, the fuck you do that for?

Murdo   You haven't got the Spartan Health company track suit on.

Donald   I'm a masseur, *I says*.

Murdo   Oh ah/

Donald   So I don't need a Spartan Health track suit.

Murdo   Are you *allowed* to not wear a track suit?

Donald   So why *did you* measure that client so thoroughly?

Murdo   Oh ah/

Donald   Why did you measure that client's *inside leg*?

Murdo   He's a new member.

Donald   He'd *already been* measured. Measured the day he joined. Charley measured him and marked it on his card.

Murdo   Only the chest and waist had been measured.

Donald   The chest and waist is all that we measure.

Murdo   Mr Bybugger said everyone had to be fully measured.

Donald   This is a busy club.

Murdo   To create uniformity.

Donald   At a busy club we measure the chest, the waist only, OK?

Murdo   But the gym was empty. (Sorry.)

Donald   But from tomorrow:/

Murdo   I had *plenty of time* to measure him fully.

Donald   Tomorrow Glasgow gets back from Tenerife.

Murdo   But the gym *wasn't* busy.

Donald   The gym *gets* busy. September starts tomorrow.

Murdo   That's great, isn't it, Mr Dick? I mean: *how* busy does it get?

Donald   *Too busy.*

Murdo   Yes, Mr Bybugger warned me. He said: 'Our Glasgow branch is hard work. But you *can* achieve.' And would you *recommend* massage, Mr Dick?

Donald   Eh? (Oh *no*. Would I fuck.)

Murdo   What, for instance, would be the role of massage in the health of the body?

Donald   (Because fuck off.)

Murdo   Because the ten-day initiation training-course at Pontefract didn't include massage. How would I go about *contacting* Mr Bybugger? I mean if I wanted to. (Pardon, sorry.)

Donald *gestures to telephone.*

Murdo   He said if I ever wanted to talk over a problem. (*Where*, sorry?)

Donald (*gesturing to telephone*)   Here, reception, *where* you want. (Fuck.)

Murdo   And I do *have* a problem.

Donald   Do you *want* to phone Bobby?

Murdo   It's to find out *exactly when* I may renew a member. (For instance.)

Donald   Because sometimes these nice bosses give it a nice touch: They go: 'Phone me with your problems.'

Murdo   But Mr Bybugger *did tell me* exactly when to renew a member.

Donald   Mr Bybugger is one busy boy.

Murdo   And I might have forgotten. I mean: I *only think* he said six visits.

Donald   A busy boy does not like to get interrupted.

Murdo   What would Mr Bybugger *do* if he *found out* I'd forgotten what he said, or *even* that I'd *got it wrong?*

Donald   So what is it with you? You some kind of boss's man? You shouldn't be a boss's man at your age, for fuck's sake. You're only a young wank. I mean I was your age I used to poke a boss's eye out with a bowling pin as soon as look at him. I used to take two-hour tea-breaks, come back tell the cunt I'd have my nooky with a poodle in a cupboard. I mean: fuck me: how come you can't wrap Bobby in kitchen foil, pop him the oven an afternoon? Because see this Bobby, right, this Bobby Bybugger thinks he's a perfect specimen? Works out, jogs, eats an immaculate diet? This/ Is all that a fact?

Murdo   Oh ah/

Donald   Aye well it's *not* a fact. When Bobby is away from home, away from Pontefract he'll eat any old garbage comes his way.

Murdo   Well I watched him in Pontefract. He never left his diet and exercise programme for a second.

Donald   That's Pontefract. Bobby is away from Pontefract a good half the year his programme gets well fucked. Hamburgers, the lot.

Murdo   In Pontefract/

Murdo *discovers empty cigarette packet.*

Donald   So my advice to you is to get to hell out of it.

Murdo   Oh ah/

Picks up cigarette packet and gives it to **Donald**.

Donald   Because you're a really nice guy. (Are you fuck.) Because see these. These belong to Charley Hood. The cunt. Aye. That's the sorry state this place has got *me* into. I was up for the priesthood before I took this job. I wouldn't have dreamed of covering up for a dirty lung-infested bastard like Charley Hood. Oh no.

Murdo   *Where* may I phone Mr Bybugger from?

Donald   Because, basically, I don't give a fuck. (Phone him where you want.) And if you want to stop *yourself* not giving a fuck get to bastarding hell out of it, before it's too late. At one point I had a twenty-eight-inch waist. I've been devastated by Spartan Health and Bobby Bybugger. I mean: I was in London before I came here. Ten scintillating years. Ample nooky, the lot. (Phone him where you want, *I says*.) And see my London pad? It was bastarding *fabulous*. I had a chandelier in my kitchenette. Now look at me.

Murdo   I'm phoning Mr Bybugger

Donald   Don't blame me and he shouts at you.

Murdo   I'm going to clear this up.

Donald   Don't forget you're *not supposed to be here yet.*

Murdo   Something's *got to be* cleared up. If Mr Bybugger/ I'll *admit* I'm here. If Mr Bybugger/ If I'm *not supposed* to be here Mr Bybugger has a right to shout at me. I *deserve* to be shouted at. But if Mr Bybugger doesn't abide by his diet and exercise programme *I don't want to be here.*

He goes to phone and thinks better of it.

I'm phoning Mr Bybugger, *in private.*

Murdo *goes out to reception.*

Pause.

Charley (*off*)   Where's that bastard?

Charley *comes on from reception.*

Bastard.

Donald *picks up phone.*

Charley   Where's that bastard?

Donald (*to* **Charley**)   Alana phoned up.

Charley   Because I get hold of Murdo and boiling his head will be too good for/ (Alana?)

Donald   Alana.

Charley   Her mother's in a coma?

Donald *shakes his head and gestures for silence.*

Charley   She's at her big Aunty Ruby's? (Oh *no*, man.)

Donald *shakes his head.*

Charley   She's over wee Gina's for a wash and a shave and a character-assassination session?

Donald *gestures for silence, firmly.*

Donald (*to phone*)   So Murdo. Get off the line, uh? I've got a very urgent business call to make for Mr Bybugger. Buzz up to you, so I will, the line's free, OK?

Donald *gestures for continued silence, he listens carefully and puts phone down.* **Donald** *gives cigarette packet to* **Charley** *who, not knowing what to do with it, puts it in his pocket.*

Charley   So where is Murdo?

Donald   Alana's phoning you back later.

Charley   What's he at reception for? (Alana? Phoning *me* back? Fuck's Alana phoning *me* back for?)

Donald   I don't know.

Charley   You should've got the number. I'd've phoned *her* back. Because *me* phoning *her* back's more my bastarding style. So where did you say she was?

Donald   I didn't.

Charley   Because where *the fuck* did you say she was? (What?)

Donald   She didn't forthcome on that.

Charley   So to bastarding fuck you jobbying shite why didn't you *make her* forthcome on that?

Pause.

So what's Murdo at reception for?

Donald   I got him out the road for you to send me in the footballer. Haw heh wait a minute: *where* is the footballer?

Charley   So the Murdo has fucked us up.

Donald   Where's my line up I says?

Charley   So that's/

Donald   Have you lost me my line up?

Charley   That's Murdo booted the night *definitely*.

Donald   Because you've lost me my line up you lousy toss off ballhead you. What are you?

Charley   *I* didn't lose you the footballer.

Donald   Oh? So who did?

Charley   Murdo.

Donald   Murdo?

Charley   Murdo! So you want to see the special-attention treatment Murdo dishes out to the footballer. Because the measurement in detail was *not* the end of it. Oh no. Also *the weight*. Also *the height*. Also the *dietary advice*. Also: the *personalised exercise programme*. I mean: is he under the presumption we are here to *serve the public*? . . . So the footballer, he goes to himself: how come I didn't get the special-attention treatment the first time I came in, the time I came to enrol, the time Charley Hood took £200 off me, measured my chest, my waist in two seconds flat? Because Donny: a place is *inconsistent* to a punter and a punter gets *alert*. And an alert bastarding punter has got an unfair advantage over us. Because an alert bastarding punter is going to *want time* to think the early renewal *over*. (Fuck.) So where is Murdo?

Donald   Eh? Oh see this Murdo:/

Charley   Because did I hear you say Murdo's phoning Bobby?

Donald   This Murdo wants to tell Bobby the way things are around here.

Charley   What've you said to Murdo?

Donald   Because Murdo is a wee boss's man that I have *almost totally* booted for us.

Charley   Because phone calls to Bobby wouldn't've arisen you had kept your gob shut, as I requested. (Fuck.)

Donald   So I *blocked* the phone call to Bobby to give you time to finish Murdo off.

Charley   Phone calls to Bobby shouldn't've arisen. I mean: you get the trust *first*. So you give the new boy a present, you give him a *promise* and you have thereafter *got his trust*. Because you have to get the trust before you can persuade the new boy he's better off fucking off.

Donald   You've lost me my footballer.

Charley   So Donny: did I say we'd *lost* the footballer? So fuck me: this Craigie Stein, right? We're sitting the sales-office he goes: 'I've got a date with a bird.' I went: 'You've got a *bigger* date with yourself, Jim.' He went: 'Oh but I'm not sure.' So I went to him: 'Sign there.' He goes: 'I've got a *date*!' I went. 'A signature costs a second.' He went: 'I want to think about it.' So the Murdo *must've* got him alert. Because a mental case with big motivation doesn't *think* about it. A mental case with a big motivation *begs* for it.

Donald   Punters walk out *don't* come back.

Charley   This is the exception, Donny.

Donald   Many's the time you've went to me: 'A punter wants it, a punter buys it *now*.'

Charley   The Craigie does want it but.

Donald   You've lost me my footballer.

Charley   No Donny. Because I went to him: 'Tonight's *the last* of the early-cheap-rate renewals.' So. He meets the bird, Donny. He meets the bird, he goes *right* off her, he'll be back. The times I've been out with a bird she's opened her gob spat out a load of wank. No Donny. He meets the bird goes off her he'll be back. Ta ra.

Donald   So I hope you do find Craigie Stein.

Charley   So do I.

Donald   I hope you find him, the bar, the Empire Hotel.

Charley   *So do I.*

Donald   I hope you find him the Alana parked his *smashed-up bastarding kneecap.*

Charley   So do/ Heh *wait* a/

Donald   Because the Alana, the Craigie *could well* have met up reception. Don't forget.

Charley   Aye could they? I mean: *could* they? (Fuck.)

Donald   Well you better find him the night.

Charley   I'll find him before the night. Because I'm going the bar, the Empire Hotel escort him back here his early-cheap-rate renewal. Then it's *over to you*, Donny boy son.

Donald   Well I *hope* you find him. These empty summer nights in Glasgow are pissing me off. And I've still got my connections in London. I could get my nooky on a regular bastarding basis there.

Charley   Aye ra ha ha cut the London garbage.

Donald   In fact: you get your nooky every fifteen seconds, the Earl's Court Road.

Charley   I've heard the London garbage before. I've/ Nooky every fifteen seconds, all the same? So give me an honorary benthood, for fuck's sake, I'll go to London, too.

Because you are one hell of a guy, Donny, the queen should get to meet you. And I love you *so* much, I wasn't so totally *not* a bent basket I'd get up your couch myself for you.

Charley *takes out cigarettes. Goes to open them. Remembers.*

Donald   And you're *not* going the bar, the Empire Hotel, by the way.

Charley   What is this?

Donald   Because what if Bobby phones back?

Charley   Bobby's *phoned* back.

Donald   What if Bobby phoned back again?

Charley   Oh fuck aye. Back again. From Pontefract.

Donald   And if he's *not* phoning you up from Pontefract:/ Because if he's not phoning you up from Pontefract you might just walk into the erratic cunt's face the bar, the Empire Hotel.

Pause.

I could go.

Charley   Pardon?

Donald   *I* could go look over the bar, the Empire Hotel.

Charley   You could? . . . You could! You go you see Craigie Stein the bar, the Empire Hotel.

Donald   So while I'm the bar, the Empire Hotel you'll boot Murdo?

Charley   Murdo?

Donald   Murdo! You'll boot him so the ugly bastard's *well gone* I get back?

Charley   I'll boot him for you Donny. Put it there.

They shake hands.

Donald   Because I don't like Murdo.

Pause.

One thing, however: I won't be the bar, the Empire Hotel long, OK?

Charley   OK.

Donald   The bar, the Empire Hotel is a shitehole.

Charley   *I know* it's a shitehole.

Donald   It's full of weirdos,/

Charley   So don't be long.

Donald   Who give me the vomit. So I won't be long, *definitely*.

Donald *picks up phone.*

Donald (*to phone*)   Murdo? . . . Mr Hood wants a word with you. (*To* **Charley**.) You ready to talk to Murdo, Mr Hood?

Charley   I'm ready, Mr Dick.

Donald (*to phone*)   What? Oh sorry, Murdo son. (*Loud to* **Charley**.) because imagine that, Mr Hood. I went *forgot* to buzz through to Murdo the line to Bobby was free. (*To* **Murdo**.) I'm not sure what he wants to talk about, Murdo. So shoot down here now, OK? . . . Let you try phoning Bobby later.

He puts phone down.

So Murdo's *right into* Bobby.

Charley   Nobody's into Bobby. That cunt's too masculine. And, I hope you kept your hands off Murdo's body, by the way.

Donald *Murdo's body?*

Charley   Because that's not what sent him upstairs, up phoning Bobby is it?

Donald   I never considered his body.

Charley   Well get a grip:/

Donald   Because his *personality* is garbage.

Charley   Because if you *don't* fancy his body you benders are getting far too bastarding fussy.

Knocking.

Donald   Heh Charley:/

Charley (*shouts*)   Holds on.

Donald   Murdo says he *wasn't* renewing Craigie.

Charley   Fuck *that*.

Donald   Bobby told him you don't renew until the sixth visit.

Charley   He measured Craigie up it wasn't needed.

Donald   He mesured him because he wasn't happy the way *you* measured him.

Knocking.

Charley   You believe that? Because Murdo might not be able to sell a renewal. But why jobby about with unreal concepts such as: 'I'm not in it for the money. I'm not in it for the nooky. I'm in it for the job satisfaction.'

Donald   I'm saying what he said.

Donald *goes out through the corridor.*

Charley   Gobble a shite. The purest vomit.

Knocking. **Charley** *takes out a cigarette packet. Goes to open it. Remembers.*

Fuck. (*Shouts, out to* **Donald**.) Heh Donny. Buy us a packet of cigarettes, uh?

Donald (*off*)   And you have got to be joking.

Knocking.

Charley (*loud*)   Come in. (*Quiet.*) For fuck's sake, *come in*.

Murdo *comes in from reception.*

Charley   Aye Murdo Caldwell? Charley Hood. Couldn't be

more pleased to meet you.

Murdo   Oh ah/

Charley   So I couldn't stop introduce myself down the gym there. The matter with the Stein punter was urgent. You saw that, you handled it *dead* professional, *dead* promising.

Murdo   Oh, ah and could I ask a question?

Charley   Ask away. I love a stimulating question. What the fuck is it?

Murdo   Oh and have you time? *You* want to talk to *me*. I mean, *do* you?

Charley   Any amount of time, can I make available, for boys the calibre of you and me. (I like it.) There's calibre in you and me companies the like of Spartan Health are bawling out for. Oh aye man, I watched you from the gym door a couple of wee minutes all impressed, hell of a impressed the gorgeous attention you gave the Stein punter . . .

Murdo   Oh ah and what did I say that was so good? (If I can know, I can keep it up.)

Charley   He almost extended his membership. Thanks to you.

Murdo   Oh? *Oh?*

Charley   So I watched you a couple of minutes, all fascinated to fuck.

Murdo   You say what *you* want *first*. (If you want.)

Charley   OK. So ra ha ha. Aye ra ha ha. I'll be showing you one of my specials. (They're brilliant.) Because a boy with talent like you:/

Murdo   Oh, ah my *talent*? What's my talent like? (Sorry.) I mean: What's your special for? Oh ah is it a 'Spartan Health' special?

Charley   It's better than *that*. (Fuck.)

Murdo   Does Mr Bybugger *not know* about it?

Charley What am I saying? It's not so much better as *equally/*

Murdo Oh ah/

Charley But if you *don't want* to try my special: I won't be insulted.

Pause.

Murdo I could try it out. I mean: couldn't I?

Charley (*severe*) So do you *want* to?

Murdo Oh, ah yes. Thank you. (Sorry.) So put it there.

They shake hands.

Pity, all the same.

Murdo Pardon?

Charley About your talent.

Murdo Oh ah what do you mean?

Charley Just the total absence of job prospects.

Murdo What?

Charley Comensurate with your talent.

Murdo (Sorry.) Because the prospects are excellent. Aren't they?

Charley And. You'll never be more than a *junior* gym instructor while I'm the senior/

Murdo I'd like to call Mr Bybugger now.

Charley Phone away.

Murdo Because everything's different from what I *expected*.

Charley (Fuck.)

Murdo And there are a number of uncleared up points.

Charley Mr Bybugger will be delighted.

Murdo *goes to phone. Thinks better of it.*

Murdo   Oh ah will he be *delighted*.

Charley   Delighted.

Murdo   Because Mr Dick thought he might be too busy to talk.

Charley   Mr Dick's got it all wrong. Mr Bybugger would be delighted to talk to you *any time*.

Murdo *goes to phone.*

Charley   I mean I can understand you wanting to talk to Bobby.

Murdo *picks up phone.*

Charley   Because Bobby – he gets me to call him Bobby – Bobby's a brilliant bloke who speaks awful well of you.

Murdo   Oh ah what does he *say*?

Charley   I can understand you wanting to talk to him.

Murdo   I mean: about me. I mean:/

Charley   You'd obviously prefer to talk to him than to talk to me.

Murdo   Oh ah/ (What?) No! I mean: 'yes'. I mean: I didn't know I *could* talk to you.

Murdo *puts phone down.*

Charley   Well I want you to know you can tell me your problems any time you like. (Fuck.)

Murdo   Is it all right?

Charley   Oh – fuck – yes.

Pause.

Charley   But it's a bastarding pity, all the same.

Murdo   Pardon?

Charley   A pity there's no decent money to pay a talent like you a decent wage, a decent commission. (Fuck.) Take me: not one sale, not one commission from a sale these two bastarding months. Because see if I was your age, son, with a talent like yours on you? . . . And. Don't think I *mean* anything by this, but if I was you I'd find myself alternative/

Murdo   Oh ah but Mr Hood: I don't *mind* if I don't do any sales.

Charley   You don't mind?

Murdo   I don't need to do any sales. (If that's all right.)

Charley   Because that's bastarding *big* of you.

Murdo   Is it? (Sorry.)

Charley   Heh, don't let's talk jobbying *wet* around here. Because we're *all* in it for the money.

Murdo   I'm not. Oh, ah would Mr Bybugger *mind*? Surely he wouldn't mind if I wasn't in it for the money. Surely he couldn't mind if Glasgow was a city of perfectly proportioned, sinuous but not overdeveloped physiques? Surely he wouldn't mind if Glasgow was a city of non-smoking, non-drinking joggers? Surely he wouldn't mind if Glasgow was a city of reposeful but alert minds? And surely he wouldn't mind if Glasgow was a wholly healthy city?

Charley   A wholly healthy Glasgow?

Murdo   Yes exactly, Mr Hood. So *do* you think he would mind?

Charley   Mind? . . . Murdo my boy son, Mr Bybugger will be delighted.

Shakes **Murdo**'s *hand.*

Because the originality of the concept is dazzling.

Murdo   I can only hope I'm big enough to achieve a Wholly Healthy Glasgow by the year 2010.

Charley   You're big enough, Murdo son. And if there's

anything I can do to help you, you know where I am.

Murdo   So *would* Mr Bybugger mind if I didn't take my equal share of the sales?

Charley   Oh no.

Murdo   Because if Mr Bybugger *insisted* I take my equal share I'd *have to* take them. (Sorry.)

Charley   Mr Bybugger *won't mind* you giving up your sales for a wholly healthy Glasgow. He'll be/

Murdo   Oh ah will I phone Mr Bybugger up and tell him?

Charley   You could do. The other hand may I make a suggestion, Murdo?

Murdo   Oh ah yes, Mr Hood.

Charley   Imagine with me, Murdo, one morning early in 2010, Mr Bybugger emerges from the Empire Hotel on the first morning of a visit to the Glasgow branch. He emerges and he sees before him a city of what was it?

Murdo   Perfectly proportioned/

Charley   Perfectly proportioned sinuous physiques. And what was it?

Murdo   Non-smoking, non/

Charley   Non-smoking, non-drinking joggers. And what was it?

Murdo   Reposeful but/

Charley   Reposeful but alert minds. Imagine it. And imagine the joy slowly appearing in Bobby Bybugger's face. And imagine how much greater that joy will be if it comes as a *complete fucking surprise.* (Employ your nut on this.) Then he would walk in here and we would be able to tell him that the wholly healthy Glasgow operation has been directed by you in the *gym* department and ably assisted by me in the *sales* department. (Am I right, am I wrong?)

Murdo　So can I ask you about my problems now?

Charley　Aye, fire away. (Fuck.)

Murdo　Were you trying to renew Mr Stein's membership on his first visit today? (Contrary to Spartan Health procedures.)

Charley　Haw heh: Craigie Stein was so impressed by you he enquired after a membership extension *himself*.

Murdo　I thought you said you tried, you *almost* renewed him.

Charley　So Mr Stein was disappointed when I had to tell him the six visits rule.

Pause.

Murdo　And Donald said maybe/

Charley　Donald?

Murdo　I mean Mr Dick. Mr Dick said you/

Charley　Because oh ho now, Murdo son, Donald. Donald is a gorgeous person. Known the bastard years. And. Utter genius at the massaging job. Not a word against him. Except. An erratic cunt, a fly shite you can't trust.

Murdo　Oh ah but I wasn't to know Donald can't be trusted. (Sorry.)

Charley　So watch what you say to Donald.

Murdo　Mr Bybugger didn't warn me.

Charley　Because he's got none of our *talent*.

Murdo　So why did Mr Bybugger *employ* Mr Dick?

Charley　Because talent does not grow on pavements. And. You go out to work every day/ If you *choose* to go out to work every day you are *surrounded by a total dearth* of talent. Oh aye: a plethora of wankers: this world, this city. (I try to act normal.)

Pause.

Murdo   So Mr Dick must have *lied* to me, Mr Hood.

Charley   A total liar, our Donny, unfortunately.

Murdo   Because Mr Dick told me you were *smoking* in here today. (Sorry.)

Charley   Me?

Murdo   Smoking, *contrary to procedures*.

Charley   So see what I mean about Donald?

Murdo   Oh ah yes, Mr Hood. And is it true Mr Bybugger eats junk food when he's away from Pontefract?

Charley   What do you think about this yourself?

Murdo   I don't think he does.

Charley   So who told you this garbage? No don't tell me:/

Charley/Murdo   Donald.

Pause.

Murdo   So I don't know if I can work with Donald. Because someone who can't be trusted might try to stop us making Glasgow a wholly healthy/

Charley   He keeps out our way, son. He stays here in his massage chambers. (His own *department!*) So not being able to trust Donald is *entirely irrelevant* . . . So is that you happy now?

Murdo   Oh ah yes.

Charley   Because you don't need to bother about Donald.

Murdo   I know Mr Hood. Because I can trust *you*. In fact, Mr Hood, I trust you *completely*.

Charley   Of course you can. Oh aye. Aye. (Fuck.)

Pause.

Murdo   But what *is* the role of massage in the health of the body?

Charley   Donny will tell you about that. In fact: he'll give you one. I'll set it up for you.

Murdo   Oh ah/

Charley   What am I saying? I've *already* set one up for you. Because, see, this special I mentioned. Guess what it is? . . . A massage! (Ta ra!)

Murdo   But I wouldn't want a massage unless it has a role in the health of the body.

Charley   When Donald – the touch – Dick is finished with you you'll be so bastarding elated you won't need to ask questions. Is that you happy yet?

Murdo   Yes. But why is the closed circuit not at reception, where it belongs?

Charley   To/ What?

Murdo   And who's that in the gym?

Murdo *goes over to the closed-circuit monitor.*

Charley   There's nobody in the gym. It's August.

He follows **Murdo** *over and looks at the screen.*

Oh, for fuck's sake, it's big Rab. Big Rab McGuigan back early from Benidorm.

Murdo   Because there's no one in the gym to give Mr McGuigan some attention.

Charley   No attention won't worry big Rab. (Fuck.)

Murdo   Could I go and give him some attention?

Charley   Oh aye. Off you go. (Fuck.)

Murdo   Oh ah thanks. (Sorry.)

He goes to go, but thinks better of it.

I'm sorry I didn't knock the door for Donald.

Charley   *What?*

Murdo   Because I'm sorry I didn't knock Donald Dick's door. (Will you have to tell Mr Bybugger?)

Charley   We'll give that one a miss, Murdo son. Don't be fretting.

Murdo   I promise I won't do it again.

Murdo *goes out to the gym.*

Charley   Oh . . . *great.*

Donald *comes in from reception.*

Donald   Right, my shagpile's dry, give me a hand down with it . . . Where's Murdo? . . . Because is that Murdo beating it already? . . . So give me a hand down with my shagpile before the footballer comes.

Charley   Where's Alana?

Donald   I've got my atmosphere to/ (What?)

Charley   Alana!

Donald   She's not the bar, the Empire Hotel.

Charley   You sure?

Donald   I'm *sure.* (Fuck.) So *has* Murdo beat it yet?

Knocking.

Pause.

Knocking.

(*Loud.*) Come in.

Murdo *comes in from the gym.*

Murdo   Oh, Mr Hood . . . Hello, Mr Dick. Mr Hood, I meant to ask you something.

Charley   Yes?

Murdo   It's because of my enthusiasm . . .

Charley   Yes, Murdo son?

Murdo   Please may I work through my lunch hours?

Long pause.

Blackout.

Act Two

Donald *and* **Charley** *come in from reception, with* **Donald**'s *carpet, which* **Donald** *arranges into place.*

Charley (*entering*)   But Donny boy, son. Your nooky will be *no* problem to Murdo . . . Because Murdo is the younger generation. And. So the younger generation have been brought up different. They are a bunch of broad-minded cunts you can't reason with.

Donald   Just leave our arrangements *exactly as they are.*

Charley   Murdo is a abnormal business opportunity.

Donald   Why can't he just beat it?

Charley   Eighteen years old and totally *not* into the acquisition of wealth yet.

Donald   I practically had him beating it.

Charley   Put your prejudice to one side, uh? (Use the bastard.)

Donald   You've no right to *risk* my nooky. Nooky's *my whole life.*

Pause.

Charley   Risk your *nooky?* Because for fuck's sake, Donny. A big bold risk might just *maximise* your nooky. I mean: from tomorrow: the Glasgow boys come rolling in off the planes. So we stick Murdo down the gym, happy keeping the members *ecstatic.* And. Meantime: I am sitting up reception *concentrating* lining you up every last possibility of nooky. So my plan enamours you?

Donald   Your plan's garbage. Backfires up your arse, I go to London.

Charley   You wouldn't go to London.

Donald   I might just *go* to London.

Charley   Fuck off to London then.

Donald   I'll go to London *if and when I choose*. I mean: what if Murdo tells Bobby?

Charley   Murdo *won't* tell Bobby.

Donald   Because Murdo and Bobby are like that. (*Gestures.*) And Bobby is an anti-bent arsehole.

Charley   I'll make sure he *doesn't tell* Bobby . . . So you *definitely* saw fuck all the bar, the Empire Hotel?

Donald   Nothing.

Charley   Good.

Donald   Fuck all, as you say.

Charley   Great. I mean: good to *know* that Alana Craigie are not *together*.

Donald   The other hand I only managed a quick look up, look down the signing in sheet.

Charley   That I am not a half-baked cunt after all. You had a quick *what*? On the *what*? Since when the bar, the Empire Hotel acquire a signing in sheet?

Donald   Reception.

Charley   Eh? Can a guy get to know what gives?

Donald   Reception, the Empire Hotel.

Charley   Reception, the Empire Hotel?

Donald   Yes.

Pause.

Charley   What for? You looked up, you looked down the signing in sheet reception, the Empire Hotel *what for*?

Donald   I've to avoid the porter.

Charley   The porter? Oh for fuck's sake, Donny. *What's going on?*

Donald   Because it's more than my life's worth to *not* avoid the porter, the Empire Hotel. Several weeks ago, right? I'm standing the bar, the Empire Hotel. This guy comes up to me. He comes up to me, he goes, 'Follow me, uh?' So I follow him out the lobby. I'm out the lobby, he's standing the lift, the back, the lift, coming across the flagrant come on. I thought, 'Fuck'. (You know.) I goes in the lift, he shuts the door, we go up, he stops it. He stops it? He *jams* it between floors. He goes, 'Take your dick out.' I goes, 'Pardon?' He goes, 'Take your dick out and *come on.*' I goes, 'What?' He goes, 'You heard.' I goes, 'OK.' After the wee episode we come out the lift *past half the bastarding staff* the Empire Hotel waiting to *get in* the lift. And. Some wise cunt goes, 'Could you credit the depths this porter guy will stoop to? Because imagine going with *that.*' So 'that' Charley is *me*. I mean: *me*? I've had *coachloads* of porters after *me* in *my* time. (Fuck.) And you want to see the uncouth the youth to me *ever since*. So see this porter, the Empire Hotel, right? I'm avoiding him.

Charley   Well ra ha ha, right enough, you kill me. And . . . And when's the date this episode?

Donald   A few weeks ago there . . . Why do you/?

Charley   Because I thought you said you weren't going to be the bar, the Empire Hotel *long*?

Donald   I wasn't long.

Charley   You *were* long. (Long as fuck.)

Donald   I wasn't long.

Charley   Bastarding ages, you were.

Donald   Was I? How long was I? Because I don't know how long I was. Do I?

Charley   Aye ra ha ha. Well ra ha ha that's you had your nooky?

Donald   I have not/

Charley   So you'll not be wanting it *again*.

Donald   I have *not* had my nooky.

Charley   You won't be wanting the footballer *now*.

Donald   I *will* he wanting the footballer. I *had better get* the footballer. Because I have not had my nooky. And even if I had had my nooky who the bastarding hell do you think you are? The nooky police?

He sits at closed circuit.

I'm occupied.

Charley   Aye ra ha ha and OK, Donny. I'll line you up the footballer as soon as he phones up. (Fuck.)

Donald   I thought he was meeting the bird, the bar, the Empire Hotel.

Charley   So did I. So I wish he'd *hurry up* and phone up.

Pause.

The Empire Hotel? The signing-in sheet? Haw heh here: how come you looked up, looked down the signing-in sheet *at all*? Because the Alana is *not* going to be hiring a room. Because the Alana's got a perfectly presentable two apartment.

Donald   She might have wanted to shack up *in style* the professional footballer.

Charley   So she can shack up in my place. My place had an interior decorator.

Donald   And I thought you wanted me to check on her.

Charley   I check on no cunt. I get her to check on *me*. (I only wanted to know she was one piece.) I'm going the bar, the Empire Hotel.

Donald   I'm occupied.

Charley *goes to go.*

Donald   And who's that in the gym?

Charley *stops, and goes to look.*

Donald   Because that looks like Murdo.

Charley   It is Murdo. (What of it?)

Donald   So what's Murdo doing talking to big Rab?

Charley   So Murdo wants to give Rab some attention.

Donald   Because no one talks to big Rab McGuigan.

Charley   So I says to him: 'OK.' (Fuck.)

Donald   And big Rab does not look happy.

Charley   Big Rab looks bastarding miserable.

Donald   Bastarding in torture.

Charley   Bastarding in agony.

Donald   So big Rab is just about to/

Charley   And oh for fuck's sake: big Rab is going to/

Donald/Charley   Big Rab's lost his temper.

Charley goes to go. Stops.

Charley   The Alana, the Craigie call get their number. I'll call them back. If it's Bobby go to him, 'Just hold on a minute.' Or, or no. Tell him to call back a wee minute, I'm in the lavvy. Or, or *definitely* no. You say I'm in the lavvy he'll go, 'Call him *out* the lavvy.' Say I'm in a sale. (Fuck.)

He goes to go. Stops himself.

And the Murdo comes up here asking for me don't, for fuck's sake, tell the cunt where I am. He'll tell Bobby.

He goes to go, feeling for cigarettes. Remembers.

So mind buy yourself cigarettes, Charley, uh?

Donald   You're *not* smoking my massage chambers.

Charley goes to go.

Donald   Because no more cigarettes my *newly cleaned shagpile* . . . And there goes Murdo with a face.

Charley *stops.*

Donald   And look *at* the face on Murdo.

Charley *crosses, looks at the screen, laughs.* **Donald** *joins him. Laughter builds and they take their attention off screen. Knocking.*

Donald (*shouts*) Come in.

Murdo *comes in from gym.*

Murdo   I'll have to leave here . . . Sorry . . . Well, Mr McGuigan is doing a non-Spartan Health work-out. He is taking rests *every ninety seconds.*

Charley   Trust Rab McGuigan to go do a non-Spartan Health work-out.

Murdo   And he said that no one had ever *tried* to *remotivate* him.

Donald   So is this you definitely leaving? I was just getting to know and love you too.

Murdo   And he said that he didn't want *anyone* to ever try remotivating him *again* . . . So he's *continuing* with his non-Spartan Health work-out.

Charley   Don't leave because of Rab, son. (Fuck.)

Murdo   *Even though* a non-Spartan Health work-out might *ruin his whole life.* Because a rest every ninety seconds could be fatal, Mr Hood. And he *swore* at me. So I'll have to definitely leave here.

Charley   A fucking bastard that Rab McGuigan. *Swearing* at Murdo.

Murdo   Everything in my gym department must go perfectly.

Charley   *So* you prefer the Spartan Health system yourself, Murdo.

Murdo   It's the *only* system.

Charley   And the Bobby tell you how to enforce it?

Murdo   Oh ah but if members are instructed correctly from the beginning.

Charley   Some these guys have been working out since long before Spartan Health work-outs were invented.

Murdo   Older members must be *re*motivated.

Charley   So how you get on with remotivating big Rab McGuigan down there?

Murdo   I wasn't to know no previous remotivational work had taken place with Mr McGuigan. (Had it?)

Charley   Because when I think the times I've went down my hands, my knees *tried* to remotivate big Rab.

Murdo   How can a man get genuinely fit *unless* he does a Spartan Health work-out?

Charley   So Murdo: you know and I know it's brilliant being fit as fuck. (Take me: I jog myself to buggery.) But a low calibre twat like Rab McGuigan cannot tell the difference between a remotivation and his wee Aunty Renee. Because all Rab wants is a waistline, a pair of shoulders and a giant prick. Get a grip, Murdo, uh? The guy's not all right the head. So I strolls in the gym one day, the Rab's wanking himself off. I goes to him: 'What the fuck do you think you're doing?' He goes, 'I'm doing my prick presses Charley.' 'I goes, 'Get to fuck you dirty cunt you.' He goes, 'My prick presses are brilliant, Charley. Fifty repetitions and you can add four inches a work-out.' . . . So, Murdo, I was just saying to Donny how it's really great the way you were tolerating Rab down there, how I really *admired* you, you know?

Murdo   Oh ah you *admired* me?

Charley   So it's a shock to learn you are one the most intolerant cunts going.

Murdo   Oh/

Charley   And I thought you were a guy with calibre could put up with a harmless half-normal ballhead doing a non-company work-out quietly the corner the gym. Yes, I admired you. However, hold on a wee minute I do an errand before you say goodbye.

Murdo   Oh ah/

Charley   In fact, Murdo gorgeous, hold on get *your massage* before you go.

Murdo   Oh ah/

Donald   His *massage*?

Charley   Because I don't bear grudges.

Donald   Who's providing the massage?

Murdo   I could try again to remotivate Mr McGuigan. Because it was my enthusiasm which made me tolerate Mr McGuigan so long.

Charley   I know: you enthusiastic cunt you.

Donald   *The massage*!

Pause.

Charley   Massage? Haw heh Murdo: that's *your* massage the Donny is referring to. And. A brilliant sense of humour, our Donny. 'Who's providing the massage?' Aye ra ha ha: who else but Donald – the touch – Dick.

Donald   (And is he fuck.)

Charley   So you will wait till I get back, Murdo son?

Murdo   Oh ah/

Charley   (Keep your gob *shut,* Donny.)

Murdo   Oh ah/

Charley   You will wait avail yourself the massage, Murdo, before you leave?

Murdo   Oh ah/

Charley   Because see you guys in a minute.

Charley *goes out to reception.*

Murdo   (I might *not* leave.)

Pause.

Thank you very much for giving me a massage, Mr Dick.

Donald   Don't thank me.

Murdo   I'm very grateful.

Donald   Because you're not fucking getting a massage.

Pause.

Murdo   Oh *why?* (Sorry.)

Donald   You just aren't.

Murdo   Don't you want to give me a massage?

Donald   No. I'm a miserable hard-hearted bastard.

Pause.

Murdo   I wouldn't mind paying.

Donald   Get to fuck.

Murdo   I mean: if I'm not *entitled to* a free Spartan Health massage, I'll pay.

Donald   I don't *want* to give you a massage, OK?

Pause.

Murdo   OK.

Long pause.

Donald   What's going on?

Murdo   Oh ah nothing.

Donald   So why don't you speak?

Murdo   Sorry. I'll try not to not speak in future.

Pause.

Donald   Oh, for fuck's sake: away home Murdo, uh?

Murdo   Oh ah do you *want* me to go home? (I *don't want* to go home. Sorry.)

Donald   Because, *as Charley says*, you're an obnoxious intolerant cunt.

Murdo   Oh but I'm not ever going to be intolerant again. Am I?

Donald   What is it with you? Ten days with Bobby Bybugger in Pontefract, you don't want to go straight home. Why?

Murdo   I don't like going home . . . I come from a problem background.

Donald   Get to fuck.

Murdo   *It is.* (Sorry.)

Donald   In what way?

Murdo   I prefer to not talk about it.

Donald   Your background can't be as big a problem as mine.

Murdo   I don't like going home to my parents. (Sorry.)

Donald   You ungrateful shite you. I haven't even got a background. I haven't even got a set of parents to *go home to*.

Murdo   Oh but, Mr Dick.

Donald   Yes?

Murdo   You don't know what it's like . . . You see my father was asked to leave the police force for drinking on duty. So he lies in bed now, *all day*. And my mother is a *very fat woman*. She gets out of breath just *climbing down the steps* to the back garden. And my sister works in a hamburger restaurant and she *eats the food*.

Donald   I see what you mean.

Murdo   So what would Mr Bybugger say if he found out?

Donald   A bastarding disaster area your background. (Mr Bybugger?)

Telephone. **Donald** *picks it up, listens and impulsively hands it over to* **Murdo**.

Ask him yourself.

Murdo (*to phone*)   Oh ah Murdo Caldwell here, Mr Bybugger.

Donald   But don't mention/

Murdo   Sorry, Mr Bybugger.

Donald   Don't mention Charley Hood.

Murdo   Oh, ah yes. 'Spartan Health. May we help you?' in future. (*To* **Donald**.) What?

Donald   Don't say Charley's gone out.

Murdo   Oh ah/

Donald   Because Bobby knows he's already had his half-hour break. So/

Murdo   Oh ah/

Donald   Just don't say Charley's gone out.

Murdo   Charley Hood's in the gym.

Donald   And don't say he's in the gym. (Oh no.)

Murdo   I can see Charley Hood on the closed circuit screen.

Donald   And can you fuck.

Murdo   I just happen to be standing by it . . . At reception, yes.

Donald   Reception? (For fuck's sake.)

Murdo   Yes, Mr Bybugger. I will.

Murdo *puts phone down.*

Donald   So sorry I shoved the phone in your face. I'm a hasty cunt.

Murdo   No. I should have been *prepared* to answer with the Spartan Health telephone procedure.

Donald   You're right. I thought it would be a brilliant test for Spartan Health telephone procedure. You failed.

Murdo   And the closed circuit *should be* at reception. I mean: what would Mr Bybugger think if he knew I was standing beside it in the *massage chambers?*

Donald   I don't know.

Murdo   I'm taking it back to reception.

Donald   Take it where the fuck you like.

Murdo   Back to reception after Mr Bybugger phones back.

Donald   Because I don't/ *Phoning back?*

Murdo   (Sorry.)

Donald   What's Bobby phoning back for?

Murdo   To talk to Mr Hood.

Donald   Oh *no.*

Murdo   Where *is* Mr Hood?

Donald   You should have said Charley was in a sale. (What?) Oh *I* don't know. (Fuck.)

Pause.

Murdo   If Mr Hood doesn't come back in time what will happen to him?

Donald   Nothing will happen to *Charley Hood. You* covered up for *him.*

Murdo   You said, 'Don't say he's gone out.'

Donald   You said he's in the gym . . . I mean, for fuck's sake, *why* the gym?

Murdo   Because oh ah I *don't know why.* I *didn't know* he *wasn't* in the gym. So what will happen to me?

Donald   Fuck it, son. You'll survive. Look at me.

Telephone rings. **Murdo** *picks it up.*

Murdo   Oh ah Spartan Health. *May we help you?* No, Mr Bybugger . . . Mr Hood *wasn't* in the gym, Mr Bybugger . . . I don't know where he is, Mr Bybugger . . . Sorry, Mr Bybugger . . . I will always tell the truth in future, Mr Bybugger . . . Bye, Mr Bybugger.

He puts telephone down.

(*To* **Donald**.) Will Mr Hood also be in receipt of a reprimand?

Donald   Och, Bobby Bybugger:/

Murdo   That's *twice* I've been shouted at.

Donald   He eats all that organic wank.

Murdo   I didn't know Mr Bybugger *shouted.* (Pardon?)

Donald   He goes about the place a daft giant muscled cunt.

Pause.

Murdo   But Mr Bybugger was right to tell me off.

Donald   So don't worry about Bobby.

Murdo   I should have been *prepared* with the telephone *procedure.* I should have told Mr Bybugger *nothing but the truth.*

Donald   He gets a kick out of *taking advantage.*

Murdo   So *I will always* tell the truth in future. (What?)

Donald   Bobby's a bastard.

Pause.

Murdo   It doesn't matter what you say about Mr Bybugger, Mr Dick. I know I can't trust you. (Sorry.)

Donald   Pardon?

Murdo   Oh, but don't worry because I know you're not all that relevant.

Donald   What?

Murdo   Mr Hood told me you're not all that relevant.

Donald   Not *relevant*?

Murdo   So it *doesn't matter* if Mr Hood and I can't trust you.

Donald   Charley Hood. (I might have known.) The lying two-sided cunt. So this means you trust Charley Hood?

Murdo   Oh ah yes. Completely.

Donald   You trust *Charley Hood*? And *completely* too? (Fuck.) Don't make me piss myself. Because when I think of the jobbying connivances I've taken from him over the years, till I'm about demented. I mean: earlier the night, an example, he lies his bastarding nut off get me get Alana out the way the Stein punter. I've told Charley, 'Give your birds peace, uh?' But, *no*. And all this for Alana. Alana, the prick in the red frock, reception. Oh but Alana: she and I go *right* back, by the way. We slag each other off on a regular basis. Talk about laugh. So she tells me the lot. Her nooky, *everything*. Where, how, who. *Who?* For fuck's sake: the porter, the Empire Hotel, Rab McGuigan, Bobby Bybugger. Don't tell Charley. Even Bobby Bybugger exploited her in Pontefract. Her on the initiation training-course, so she was. Oh aye. Alana's lifestyle's fabulous. Charley Hood tells you not to trust me? (I mean: *me*!) I am one the most put upon cunts going. So come on to fuck, Murdo, son.

Murdo   I thought there was *something* wrong with Charley Hood. Because he let me off/

Donald   *Something*?

Murdo   He let me off lightly when I told him I didn't knock your door.

Donald   Eh?

Murdo   I don't like a lack of thoroughness like that.

Donald   Of course you don't.

Murdo   A knocking doors rule ought to be adhered to.

Donald   Exactly. (Fuck.)

Murdo   And may I ask a question?

Donald   Oh God, aye.

Murdo   What is the role of massage in the health of the body?

Donald   Massage?

Murdo   Massage!

Donald   Absolutely sweet fuck all.

Murdo   But Mr Hood told me it had an *important* role. And *you* would tell me about it.

Donald   Not at all.

Murdo   *Yes*! Because if massage had an important role in the health of the body Mr Bybugger would have *definitely* included it in the initiation training course. Wouldn't he?

Donald   So you'll now have to leave, won't you?

Murdo   Mr Bybugger would never have *exploited* Alana in Pontefract. I mean: how do you know Alana didn't want to experiment with *him*?

Donald   The exploitation was unadulterated.

Murdo   But Mr Bybugger is a genuine human being and very forward-looking.

Donald   Is he fuck.

Murdo   Very broad-minded, open in every way and bisexual.

Donald   Is he definitely fuck. Bobby Bybugger does not entertain bent goings on.

Murdo   He does.

Donald   A deplorable attitude for this day and age. I mean: two guys meet the club take a justifiable interest to shag each other stupid. Wanting it the now. None of your hanging about till their nobs drop off. Bobby would shoot them up the cunt before he'd let them employ his premises. (Fuck.)

Murdo   I *agree* with the no-sex-on-the-premises rule.

Donald   The/

Murdo   Because unchecked sex-on-the-premises would tend to *discourage* new members from joining and existing members from renewing.

Donald   Who's going to enforce a no-nooky rule a building this size?

Murdo *picks up closed-circuit monitor.*

Murdo   Someone will have to *try* to enforce it.

Murdo *makes to go out via reception.*

Donald   So you know you said you were beating it?

Murdo *stops.*

Donald   I'd beat it if I was you.

Murdo *continues.*

Murdo *stops himself.*

Murdo   But what do you think of the no-sex-on-the-premises rule, Mr Dick?

Donald   Yes?

Murdo   Don't you mind me taking the closed-circuit monitor back?

Donald   No.

Murdo   Back to reception?

Donald   No.

Murdo   Back to *where it belongs?*

Donald   Because *definitely* no.

Murdo *continues.*

Murdo *stops himself.*

Murdo   And if I leave here who will be left to enforce Spartan Health rules? Do you think I could tolerate *not trusting anyone*? . . . I mean: is it *relevant* that I also don't trust Charley Hood?

Charley *comes in from reception.*

Donald   Bobby phoned.

Charley   And?

Donald   Murdo covered for you.

Charley   Murdo cov/ ?

Donald   But then Bobby phoned back.

Charley   Covered for *me?* What?

Donald   And found out Murdo was lying.

Pause.

Charley   Thanks, son.

Murdo   Don't thank me.

Charley   And don't worry about Bobby.

Murdo   I won't.

Charley   Because I'll look after Bobby for you.

Murdo   Oh, don't say anything to Mr Bybugger.

Charley   I'll put in a helpful word.

Murdo   Please.

Charley   The least I can do. (Fuck.)

Murdo   Don't! . . . Because I didn't *intend* to help you. If you shouldn't've been out I wouldn't've helped you if I'd *known* you shouldn't've been out. I was confused. (Sorry.)

Murdo *goes out to reception with closed-circuit monitor.*

Charley   So Donny: guess who's the Empire Hotel, uh? . . . No *wait* a wee minute. (*Shouts off to reception.*) Heh Murdo: Where you going?

Murdo (*off*)   I'm returning the monitor to reception.

Charley (*to* **Donald**)   Thank fuck for that.

Murdo (*off*)   Where it belongs.

Charley (*shouts off*)   Back down here right after, uh? Because we're doing you the massage the now.

Murdo (*off*)   Oh ah *now?* (Why?)

Charley (*shouts off*)   The now and *come on.*

Murdo (*off*)   But Donald doesn't want to give me one.

Charley   Fuck you said, Donny?

He fumbles for cigarettes. Remembers.

(Because *fuck*.) (*Shouts off.*) Aye he *does*.

Murdo   He said he didn't.

Charley (*shouts off*)   So get ready, uh? (What?)

Murdo   You don't Mr Dick, do you?

Donald *shakes his head.*

Donald   No, I do not/

Charley *covers* **Donald***'s mouth.*

Charley (*shouting off, improvising* **Donald***'s voice*)   I was only pulling your leg earlier, Murdo son. I'd love to give you a massage. Be gorgeous.

Murdo (*off*)   Oh ah no thanks. (*Further away.*) Because massage does not have an important role in the health of the body.

Charley (*quiet*)   Fuck that.

Murdo (*off*)   Thanks. (*Gone.*)

Charley *releases* **Donald**.

Donald   And if you think I was wasting my time, my labour giving Murdo one of my good massages, when he *definitely won't* accept my nooky-on-the-premises/

Charley   He *won't*? Because how come you *know* he won't? . . . I told you *not to* bring it up. I mean do your jobbying *calculations*, Donny. The massage's *the lever* we're using *get him accept* your nooky.

Pause.

Donald   So who was at the Empire Hotel?

Charley   Not Alana. Not Craigie Stein. But I took my time, looked up, looked down the signing in sheet . . . and found: *Bobby Bybugger's* signature. (Ta ra) . . . So the morrow Bobby will *definitely* walk in here. So. That's you *definitely* giving Murdo a massage.

Donald   Am I fuck.

Charley   Because you don't give Murdo a high quality massage – I report your nooky to Bobby the morrow morning.

Donald   So Bobby boots me and who takes my place?

Charley   Murdo.

Pause.

Donald   Murdo might leave.

Charley   Murdo does not intend to leave. (I am not a fuckwit.)

Donald   Murdo can't massage.

Charley   He can learn massage. (Because fuck all to it.)

Donald   He won't accept you raking in all the cash.

Charley   He *has* accepted it . . . Because he trusts me completely.

Pause.

Donald   You couldn't operate without me.

Charley   Who couldn't?

Donald   I will not be degraded by your vicious low-down blackmail.

Charley   Because it is time to expand your vision. An instructor the gym expands my money, expands your nooky, expands our/

Donald   I will not be bribed while you run me down behind my back. Massage a cunt's been told a pack of disgusting lies about me.

Charley   What the fuck's Murdo said next?

Donald   My dignity in tatters.

Charley   Because Murdo will have to learn to *not* talk behind our backs about *us* talking behind our backs. And Donny: get a grip, for fuck's sake.

Donald   I'm the sensitive type. (At times.)

Charley   So we boot each other the balls it's *OK*. It's for the long-term *communal* gain.

Donald   I want my nooky.

Charley   And I want my renewal.

Donald   And I am not doing this massage unless you *guarantee* me my nooky.

Charley   So you're not big enough take a risk, uh?

Donald   A guarantee, *I says.*

Telephone.

Charley   Aye ra ha, you kill me.

He picks up telephone.

'Guarantee me my nooky.' . . . (*To phone.*) Spartan Health.

May we help you? . . . (*To* **Donald**.) It's the voice of . . . your nooky. (*To phone.*) Hello there, Mr Stein . . . (*To* **Donald**.) You nooky *guaranteed*. (*To phone.*) Where? Who? . . . Yes, because *oh* yes, Mr Stein . . . In fact, I'll check for you.

He holds up two fingers to **Donny**.

(*Loudly to* **Donny**.) How many these early-cheap-rate renewals we got left, Mr Dick?

Holds phone towards **Donald**.

Donald (*very loud*)   Two, Mr Hood.

Charley *shakes his head.*

Charley (*loud*)   And will head office allow us to hold any of them for Mr Stein here till the morning, Mr Dick?

Donald (*very loud*)   I'm afraid not, Mr Hood.

Charley (*very loud*)   And how soon are they likely to be sold, Mr Dick?

Donald (*loud*)   Oh ah/

Charley *holds two fingers very close.*

Donald   They could go any time, Mr Hood.

Charley (*to* **Donald**)   Thank you, Mr Dick. (*To phone.*) Did you hear that, Mr Stein? . . . See you in twenty minutes, Mr Stein.

He puts phone down.

Pause.

So Donny: that's your nooky guaranteed *definitely*. The Stein punter *does* meet the wee bird, the Empire Hotel. But she wants to go a curry. They *leave* the Empire Hotel. A taxi across town some curry-house she fancied. They sit down. They order. She goes the lavvy. Several minutes pass. She does not come back the lavvy. Half an hour passes. He realises he has had the boot in a big way. The boot in a big way? The *anti-climax* in a big way. So he is paying the bill, he is taxiing back

here. Alone. So Donny. After the high-quality massage, we get
Murdo brought round on nooky, I will line you up the
footballer. (Not that you deserve it: you obstacle-
manufacturing cunt you.)

Donald   Right. Twenty minutes high-quality massage. Not
a second more.

Charley *feels for cigarettes. Remembers.*

Charley   I'll go out buy a packet of cigarettes, uh Donny?

Donald   You're not smoking here, flicking my shagpile, I've
got a line up coming.

Charley   You're right. Because I get Murdo down, go back
out, meanwhile you try the hand with Murdo that's us well
fucked.

Charley *goes to phone.*

Donald   You have *got to be* joking. Nooky with Murdo? I'd
go, 'Have you come yet?' He'd go, 'Oh ah I didn't know I
could come. I haven't asked Mr Bybugger's permission.' And
my taste is *not in my arse*, is it?

Charley   You tell me.

He picks up phone, listens, puts it down.

Murdo was on the line.

Pause.

Donald   Who to?

Charley   I didn't want to listen in. *Did* I?

Donald   Why the fuck not, for fuck's sake?

Charley   Because I am not a nosey demoralising bag of
crumpled shite like you, am I?

Donald *picks up telephone, listens and puts it down.*

Donald   Murdo's off the line.

Charley   Murdo was on the line.

Donald   He's off the line *now*.

Charley *picks it up, listens and puts it down.*

Charley   So what was he *doing* on the line?

Donald   I don't know. (Fuck.)

Charley   Because what did you say made him *want* to go on the line?

Donald   Nothing. Not a thing.

Pause.

Charley/Donald   So where the fuck *is* he?

Telephone rings.

Donald *picks up phone, listens, quickly passes it over to* **Charley**.

Charley (*to phone*)   Spartan Health. May we help you?

Donald   *I'll* find Murdo. (Fuck.)

Donald *goes out to reception.*

Charley (*to phone*)   Well hello *again*, Mr Stein.

Donald (*off*)   And you had better line me him up.

Charley   (*You'll* be lucky you get a boot up the/) So Mr Stein, where/ ? . . . You're *still* at the curry house? . . . You trouble getting a taxi, I suppose? . . . Oh, so the wee bird turned up? (Fuck.) Uh? I mean you were just about to leave . . . you heard a scream, she was locked the lavvy . . . What a comical sound that must have/ . . . Aye ra ha ha, and I can just picture it . . . (Fuck.) . . . So that you on your way round here now, uh? . . . Oh the wee bird want to go a bevvy the bar, the Empire Hotel first?

Donald *comes in from reception, 'in haste', unseen by* **Charley**.

Charley   So after your wee drink, Mr Stein, you maybe like pop over? I believe we do still have *one* early-cheap-rate renewal remaining . . . Oh, ah bye, Mr Stein.

We understand that **Mr Stein** *has hung up.*

Donald   'Bye, Mr Stein.'

Charley *drops the phone violently on to the receiver.*

Charley   Oh mammy, daddy, Donny don't/

Donald   That you lost me my footballer again?

Charley   Don't *do* that.

Donald   Because no footballer/

Charley/Donald   No massage.

Charley   I know. And.

Pause.

Donald   And no Murdo, no massage.

Charley   So where is he?

Donald   Why don't we just boot him?

Charley   Where is Murdo and *come on?*

Donald   I almost had him booted at one point.

Charley   Murdo is *not* getting booted.

Donald   Because he is one of the most unpredictable pricks I've encountered.

Pause.

Charley   So he's not reception?

Donald   He's not *the building*.

Charley   He's not the gym?

Donald   I checked him the closed circuit.

Charley   He's not the lavvy?

Donald   He's not the lavvy.

Charley   How do you know he's not the lavvy?

Donald   He's not the lavvy!

Charley   Because the closed circuit does not *show* the lavvy. (Thank fuck.)

Donald   He's not the lavvy, because let's face it about Murdo: Murdo does not *go* the lavvy.

Pause.

Charley   Uh? Oh *aye*. Aye ra ha ha, you kill me. OK, where *is* Murdo?

Donald   I don't/

Knocking.

Pause.

Charley   You going to do the massage?

Donald   Am I fuck.

Charley   OK, Donny. No bastarding massage. Because do you think I can't get Murdo brought round *without* a massage? Because I can do any bastarding thing I choose with Murdo. You can keep your gob shut.

Knocking.

Donald   I think I'll just go to London.

Charley   Aye, go to London, for fuck's sake. (*Loud.*) Come in. (*Quiet.*) Go to London, give us all peace.

Murdo *comes in from reception.*

Donald   Where have you been?

Charley   (We were just wondering.)

Murdo   The Empire Hotel.

Charley   Oh, the Empire Hotel?

Donald   What the fuck for?

Murdo   I was looking for Mr Bybugger. (Sorry.)

Pause.

Donald   How did you know he was at the/?

Charley   Did you find him?

Murdo   I phoned up Pontefract and they/

Charley   Did you find him?

Donald   You'd no fucking right to phone up Pontefract.

Murdo   Yes, I found him.

Charley   You did, uh? (Fuck.) So what did you say to him?

Murdo   Nothing.

Donald   I might've wanted to phone up Pontefract. (Nothing?)

Charley   You said *nothing*?

Murdo   Mr Bybugger wouldn't *let me* say anything. And Mr Bybugger was eating a sausage. I don't mind if you two eat a sausage, because I know I can't trust *you two*. But if Mr Bybugger's eating a sausage who *can* I trust? And then he told me off for drinking on duty, when I wasn't drinking on duty. I was only going to look for Mr Bybugger to find out if it was *all right* not to trust you two.

Charley   You definitely said nothing?

Murdo   I didn't get a chance to. I didn't know Mr Bybugger was such an angry person. Yes, he told me off for drinking on duty and sent me back here.

Donald   You're not on duty but.

Murdo   Oh ah Mr Bybugger was quite right:/

Donald   And you *weren't* drinking.

Murdo   I volunteered to work. And I placed myself in incriminating circumstances just being *in* the bar, the Empire Hotel.

Donald   So I'd just beat it if I was you.

Murdo   So I don't know what I'm going to do. (Pardon?)

Donald   You might as well beat it.

Murdo   Oh, I can't do that.

Donald   Why not?

Murdo   If I left what about a wholly healthy Glasgow?

Charley   Exactly.

Pause.

Donald   What is this?

Murdo   Oh yes, Mr Dick. A wholly healthy Glasgow by 2010.

Donald   What's going on?

Charley   And I'm helping you, Murdo son, aren't I?

Donald   Don't talk shite.

Charley   Whether you like it or not, Donald, a wholly healthy Glasgow by 2010. That right, Murdo?

Murdo   That's right, Mr Hood. (If possible.)

Donald   Bobby won't like a wholly healthy Glasgow.

Charley   Bobby will be delighted. Won't he, son?

Murdo   Yes. And we're keeping it as a surprise for him.

Charley   And you won't get in our way, Donny, will you?

Murdo   Oh ah how could Mr Dick get in our way if he sticks to his own department?

Donald   I won't be getting in your way. (Fuck.) I might go to London.

Charley   Exactly, son: he'll stick to his own department. Or even better: he'll fuck off to London.

Donald   But I'd leave if I was you, Murdo.

Murdo   Oh ah why?

Charley   Pay no attention, son. In fact: let's get to fuck out of here, out the cunt's department . . . You coming?

Murdo   Why should I leave, Mr Dick?

Donald   Because . . . /

Charley   Donny!

Donald   Because I'm bent.

Charley   (Oh for *fuck's* sake.)

Donald   Bent as fuck.

Charley   Don't listen to him.

Murdo   Oh, I don't mind, Mr Dick.

Charley   Don't pay/ (What?)

Murdo   I don't mind if you are a homosexual, Mr Dick. I quite like you.

Donald   That's bastarding unfortunate, Murdo. Because, quite frankly, *you* give *me* the vomit.

Pause.

Charley   Aye ra ha ha, right enough, you kill me Donny. So Murdo, I can see this tolerance is a massive part of you.

Murdo   Oh yes, I'm very tolerant now, Mr Hood, thanks to you.

Charley   Of course you are. Your tolerance is prominent.

Donald   And not only am I bent, Murdo:/

Charley   (Donny!) Your tolerance is/

Donald   I'm bent on the premises.

Pause.

Charley   So, as I was saying, Murdo son, if you are genuinely intent on getting a wholly healthy Glasgow you will encounter a lot of the flying wank of life on the journey, so you will. And/

Murdo   Is this true, Mr Dick?

Donald   True as fuck.

Charley   Who can say if it's true?

Donald   Because see me: I am one the lowest quality cunts the world. Because there is not one guy going I haven't had my hand *well down* his trousers. (On the premises.)

Pause.

Charley   Fascinating thing is, Murdo, I have never yet *seen* one these disgusting acts Donny says he commits.

Murdo   Mr Dick is either breaking the rules or he isn't. *Which?*

Donald   I am.

Charley   He isn't.

Murdo   Well I don't trust either of you. So I don't know who to believe.

Donald   So I'd leave if I was you.

Murdo   If it's true I'll have to leave . . . Mr Hood?

Charley   Yes, Murdo son?

Murdo   Why would Mr Dick lie about this?

Charley   Some these washed-up benders, they'll say anything impress you. (Impress theirselves.) 'Oh aye,' Donny goes, 'I've just this minute kissed a plumber's nipple!' The finger to it, son, take pity, thank fuck you me we're not like that. However, you obviously don't want a wholly healthy Glasgow badly enough.

Murdo   I do.

Charley   Not *enough*.

Donald   Aye. You don't enough. (Fuck.) You'd better go.

Murdo   OK. I'll go.

Pause.

Charley   A pity, all the same, you couldn't tolerate a few Donny's indiscreetnesses, even if he *does* do them.

Donald   I do do them.

Charley   Even if he does do them. A pity a really great *end* like a wholly healthy Glasgow should get fucked because you, sir, rate yourself well above the admittedly disgusting *means*.

Murdo   But if Mr Dick has sex-on-the-premises new members will be discouraged from/

Donald   Exactly.

Charley   Not at all.

Murdo   And existing members from/

Donald   Exactly, *I said*.

Murdo   Existing members from/

Charley   Murdo?

Murdo   Yes.

Charley   May I say something here?

Murdo   *Oh* yes, Mr Hood.

Charley   I'd like you to imagine what it's like to be old.

Donald   What do you know about 'old'?

Charley   I know.

Donald   You're not old.

Charley   I am old. Old and decrepit compared to young Murdo here. And I have to say old cunts like me get sensations young cunts know fuck all about, Murdo. Take knackered, take frustrated, take demoralised. Take *what the fuck you like*. So you're knackered, frustrated, demoralised and in for a work-out one night, you walk into Donald – the touch – Dick. Aye, you walk into him a state of imminent collapse, he offers you a large dod of *release*, you jump at it. (Fuck.) Don't you? Because what Donald offers *is* release. Release? It's not release: it's pure jobbying *therapy*. Other words, an antidote that bogging shitehole a city out there. And. So see this therapy, right? This therapy should take pride of place in any scheme make Glasgow a wholly healthy city. So, for fuck's sake, Murdo, you stroll into the massage chambers, one afternoon, by chance, it happens to the lot of us, you stroll into the massage chambers one afternoon halfway to a wholly healthy Glasgow recognise the apparently disgusting vision you see before you for what it really is: *therapy*.

Donald   Is it fuck therapy. It's a pornophallic half-baked grope the dark, you don't know what hot wet object you'll put your hand on *next*.

Charley   Half up his own arse with terminology, Murdo. But it's the *effect* of Donny's work in therapy concerns you me, Murdo. Us wholly healthy Glasgwegians.

Murdo   If this therapy has a role in the health of the body why wasn't it included in the ten-day initiation training-course?

Donald   Exactly.

Murdo   So if this therapy were to be included in a wholly healthy Glasgow we'd have to ask Mr Bybugger's *permission* first. (Sorry.)

Charley   You feel you can *trust* Bobby Bybugger about therapy and a wholly healthy Glasgow do you?

Murdo   Oh ah/

Charley   Because, Murdo: has Bybugger ever lied to you?

Murdo   Oh ah/

Charley   *Has* he?

Murdo   Yes. (Sorry.)

Charley   The sausage?

Murdo   Yes. The sausage.

Charley   Well, don't worry about Bobby lying *to you*. Because Bobby has also lied *to me*.

Murdo   Oh, what lie/?

Charley   OK, I'm at Pontefract. Bybugger goes: 'You ya
cunt. Dare renew anybody pre-sixth visit you're booted.' So I
get back to Glasgow, I discover this talent I've got for
enrolling, renewing in practically the same bastarding breath.
So OK, I admit it: I totally ignore the six-visits rule. See any
sign Bobby saying no to all the cash I bring him in.

Murdo   Is this true? . . . Mr Dick, is this true?

Donald   Get to fuck, Murdo. You don't trust me.

Charley   Thank fuck for which.

Murdo   Because I thought the six-visits rule was *essential* to
give the member *time to understand the value* of the early cheap-
rate renewal.

Charley   Is it fuck. The six-visits rule is because Bybugger
assumes his staff are a load of untalented zombie ignoramuses.
That have to show two inches off their fat arse first. That can't
even make the stupid cunts of members' minds up for them!
So, Murdo: you going to get out the streets fight for a wholly
healthy Glasgow or toss yourself off in the feet asking Bobby
Bybugger's permission?

Murdo   Oh ah/

Charley   A wholly healthy Glasgow or a broken-backed
wanker like Bobby Bybugger? Which?

Murdo   Does this mean I can't trust Mr Bybugger or, or
anybody?

Charley   Which?

Murdo   Oh ah/

Donald   Aye, *which*, for fuck's sake.

Charley   Which.

Pause.

Murdo   A wholly healthy Glasgow.

Charley   Congratulations.

Donald   Biggest fuck up your life that decision.

Charley   That's 'Donald' for 'A very impressive move there, Murdo son gorgeous.'

Murdo   Oh, ah but in what ways is Mr Bybugger a broken-backed wanker?

Charley   Well, son. Say a punter begs him accept £200 cash, he goes: 'Sure you wouldn't like a *couple of years* think it over?'

Donald   Aye. And he's a/

Charley   Or. He takes on 50p-a-week punters that *don't come back.*

Donald   And he's a/

Charley   Or. He gives it away *free* he likes the sight their tit.

Donald   And he's a useless fuck.

Charley   Of course he is. Exactly. Who told you?

Murdo   Mr Bybugger is not a useless fuck.

Charley   Who told you?

Murdo   Mr Bybugger is not a useless fuck, I said . . . Because/

Charley   Donny: *who told you*?

Donald   Alana told me.

Charley   Who told Alana?

Murdo   Because I experimented sexually with Mr Bybugger.

Pause.

Donald   I *thought* you were half bent.

Murdo   Are *you* tolerant of sexual experimentation, Mr Hood?

Donald   Very tolerant is our Charley. Aren't you, son?

Murdo   And are *you* tolerant of sexual experimentation, Mr Dick?

Donald   Get to fuck. I'm sorry, but I'm old-fashioned.

Pause.

Charley   You miserable bastard you, Donald Dick.

Donald   Don't you 'miserable bastard' me, Charley Hood. I've been *good* to you: I kept the Alana Bobby secret all these years. It takes a Murdo arrival before *that* comes out.

Charley   (Years?)

Pause.

Murdo, son.

Murdo   Yes, Mr Hood.

Charley   Do me a favour, uh? Go see you can see Craigie Stein the bar, the Empire Hotel, uh?

Murdo   I don't mind going for you, Mr Hood. But what if Mr Bybugger sees me?

Charley   Don't go *right in* the bar. Stay *the doorway*. Take *a look*.

Murdo   And what if I do see Mr Stein?

Charley   Just come back and tell me. Tell me he's alone, who he's with, *whatever*. (Fuck.)

He fumbles for cigarettes as **Murdo** *goes to go.* **Charley** *remembers.*

In fact: *fuck* . . . So, Murdo: pick us up a packet of cigarettes, uh?

Murdo   You don't smoke, Mr Hood.

Murdo *goes out to reception.*

Donald   'You don't smoke, Mr Hood.'

Charley   Alana and Bobby?

Donald   I don't think I'll *ever* like Murdo.

Charley   Bobby and Alana?

Donald   So, I'll maybe just go to London.

Charley   Bobby and *Alana?*

Donald   But when I think of the years I've spent accumulating these massage chambers: my shagpile, my atmosphere, my nooky.

Charley   My Alana . . . Where *is* my Alana?

Donald   But I'll *have to* go to London *now.*

Charley   You'll *have* to/? No you *won't* have to go to London.

Donald   I do.

Charley   Because I got Murdo brought round.

Donald   Because I'll *never* get used to Murdo.

Charley   But *Murdo's brought round* on your nooky, I says. (Fuck.)

Donald   I'm going to London.

Charley   Don't act it. You wouldn't go/ London? . . . *London?* I've *got* it, Donny boy son: I'll come to London *with* you.

Donald   Fuck off.

Charley   Because what does it *feel like* being a bastarding disgusting bender?

Donald   Aye and you came to London with me the Earl's Court Road would empty in two seconds flat.

Charley   Aye would it? Because *will I fuck* come to London with you. London? That shiting esoteric wankhole down south. And. Don't come it, Donny boy son. You're not going to London. Because London doesn't *give a fuck*. I mean: you're staggering home some Saturday night swearing your nut off

you didn't get your nooky. What cunt's going to stop take time
give you the bat the mouth you deserve? Uh? London?
London: nooky every fifteen seconds? I pissed my pants. Aye
London: who the fuck would *have* you?

Donald   I had a fabulous life in London.

Charley   London! All you get London's stockbrokers,
artistic directors, Members of Parliament, perverts like that.

Donald   I am so bastarding nooky-less, a Member of
Parliament would do me fine.

Charley   Whereas Glasgow, Donny, *Glasgow* you get your
pick the broke-down wee runt footballers never washed their
feet their lives. (Thanks to me.)

Donald   I want my nooky.

Charley   OK. Because I want my renewal. My renewal? I
want my Alana . . . Where is Alana?

Donald   I don't know, Charley. But *if* she's with the
footballer she's probably having a *fabulous* time.

Charley   Oh Donny boy, son, don't/

Donald   And if she *is* with him I suppose I might have to
end up making do with her telling me *how* fabulous it was,
afterwards.

Charley   Oh don't say that, Donny.

Donald   Things bad, uh?

Charley   Donny, son.

Donald   Because don't worry.

Charley   Donny boy, son. Things are/

Donald   Because the way things are going for you, Charley
Hood, they'll get a lot worse *yet*.

Charley   Thanks, Donny.

Donald   Don't mention it. I don't know how you can't just
find yourself some other bird.

Charley   I am not finding another bird.

Donald   Because there's plenty them going about.

Charley   Where else am I going to get a bird you have to send a search party out for every other night?

Murdo (*off, on tannoy*)   Instructor to reception. Instructor to reception, please. Thank you.

Charley   Did someone speak?

Murdo (*off on tannoy*)   Instructor to reception please.

Donald   You heard it.

Charley   No way do I answer that.

Donald   *Don't you dare* answer that.

Charley   Because Murdo will have to/

Murdo (*off, on tannoy*)   Charley Hood to/ Oh ah will Charley Hood proceed directly to the *gym* please. The new member will be waiting for you there.

Charley   *What* new member?

Donald   What *next*?

Charley   Maybe Donny, we should get Murdo to beat it, *after all*?

Donald *turns slowly to* **Charley**.

Murdo *comes in from reception, carrying the closed-circuit monitor. He has two sheets of paper tucked into his track suit bottoms.*

Murdo   Mr Bybugger has apologised for shouting at me. He didn't need to. And he thinks I'm a 'great guy with a great future'.

Charley   You weren't supposed to go *in* the bar, the Empire Hotel.

Murdo   Oh, but I did, Mr Hood. To pick up your cigarettes.

He produces and gives **Charley** *his cigarettes.* **Charley** *takes them.* **Murdo** *sets up monitor during next speech.*

Didn't I? . . . Because I can tolerate *anything* now. I'm even going to tolerate you smoking on the way to a wholly healthy Glasgow. Mr Bybugger thinks a wholly healthy Glasgow is a wonderful publicity idea, by the way. So, you needn't worry about him. He's also very interested in your therapy, Donald. He's considering including it in the ten-day initiation training-course.

Charley   What's that?

He snatches one of the sheets from **Murdo**.

Heh. This is a *renewal contract*. What the fuck's/?

Murdo   Oh ah Mr Bybugger persuaded Mr Stein to renew.

Charley   Mr Stein?

Murdo   Yes.

Charley (*verifying it*)   Craig Duff Stein. (Fuck.) Wait a minute. (*Looking elsewhere in the contract.*) It says: 'Signed by: Murdo Caldwell'.

Murdo   Yes. Mr Bybugger asked me to *finish off* his renewal.

Charley   That was *my* renewal.

Murdo   Because Mr Bybugger wanted to finish off a *new* enrolment.

He produces the other sheet of paper.

I sent him on down to the gym, for you.

Charley *glances at it.*

Murdo   And I enjoyed finishing off Mr Stein's renewal. Helping him decide.

Charley (*attending to new sheet*)   Free? A free one? What's going on?

Donald *settles down in front of closed-circuit monitor.*

Murdo   Oh ah Mr Bybugger is in a very *generous* mood.

Charley   Generous with my livelihood.

Donald   With my nooky.

Murdo   And a very happy mood.

Charley   Happy? See you Murdo, you/

Murdo   And Mr Bybugger says I'm a very talented salesman. And that I *don't* have to stick to the gym department. Oh, yes. I can sell or do therapy if I like.

Charley   You Murdo are/

Murdo   And he said that you're quite right, Mr Hood. The six-visits rule *is* for untalented staff only.

Charley   I have only one thing left to say to you.

Murdo   I've *never seen* Mr Bybugger in such a wonderful mood.

Charley   Fuck you.

Donald   Oh ho.

Charley   And fuck you rigid.

Donald   Ah huh.

Murdo   So he gave me the night off to prepare for my first big day tomorrow . . . Oh yes a much better mood. Because he said to me that sometimes Glasgow is a very surprising place, a very experimental place and then he winked at me as he got into the lift with Alana and Mr Stein. What did that mean, do you think?

He goes to go.

Charley   So, Murdo.

Murdo *stops.*

Murdo   Yes?

Charley   You're not really thinking of sticking around this back alley health joint?

Murdo   Oh ah yes, Mr Hood.

Charley   Because Spartan Health/ Because Bobby
Bybugger is a a a a rusting redundant vasectomy in a
refrigerated dildo. A diabolical floating shite in a/

Murdo   Mr Hood. Don't waste your breath.

Charley   In a/

Murdo   I *know* all that.

Charley   In a/

Murdo   And I'm taking it in my stride because I'm so
enthusiastic, so tolerant, so committed to a wholly healthy
Glasgow.

Donald   Would that kind of talk not just give you the vomit?

Murdo   And because you, because you *two* are so irrelevant.

He goes out to reception, repeating 'Irrelevant, irrelevant, irrelevant'.

Charley   So therefore, Donny, this Murdo character has no
normal human feelings for me to take advantage of . . . Has
he?

Donald   Get to fuck.

Charley *lights cigarette, takes a puff.*

Charley   So what are you looking at *now*?

Donald   Nothing.

Charley   Because whatever you're looking at/

Charley *goes to spin chair, with less energy than before.* **Donald**
turns and prevents him, sees cigarette.

Donald   But get that cigarette out.

Charley *takes a puff.*

Donald   Because I've got my shagpile to think about.

Charley   Oh, see your shagpile:/

Donald   The cigarette.

Charley   Certainly.

Charley *stubs the cigarette out systematically with his foot, in the shagpile.*

Donald *turns away and adjusts closed circuit.*

Donald   Who's that the gym?

Charley *looks.*

Charley   Fuck knows.

Donald   Oh God, help me. It's the porter, the Empire Hotel.

Charley   Aye ra ha ha, you kill me. So after I renew this porter guy, want me to line him up the après-massage?

Donald   Don't you mean the therapy?

Charley   I/

Donald *stabs adjustment to the closed circuit.*

Charley   So tomorrow, Donny, new plans.

Donald   Get to hell.

Charley   New plans get rid the new instructor.

Donald   I'm all right as I/

Charley   Tomorrow.

Charley *spins* **Donald**'s *chair and exits.*

Donald   I'm/ I'm/ I'm/

Chair stops.

I'm occupied.

American Bagpipes

American Bagpipes was first performed at the Royal Exchange Theatre, Manchester, on 4 February 1988. The caset was as follows:

Rena Nauldie   Eileen Nicholas
Sandra Michigan   Eliza Langland
Willie Nauldie   Campbell Morrison
Patrick Nauldie   Tom Mannion

Directed by Casper Wrede
Designed by Geoff Rose

Characters

Rena Nauldie, *late fifties*
Sandra Michigan, *her married daughter, mid thirties*
Willie Nauldie, *her husband, late fifties*
Patrick Nauldie, *her son, late twenties*

Setting

The living room of the Nauldie home. Pale blue or light-coloured carpet. Well worn. A couple of gaps at the side. Stained and worn areas should be arranged in preparation to be concealable by furniture.

Act One

Lights come up on room stripped of furniture except upright chairs, cleaned ironed police shirt and tea on one gap in the carpet. Phone with cable on another. **Sandra** *comes in from the street, wearing coat and carrying parcels.*

Sandra   Well, that taxi definitely came a long way round, Mother.

Rena (*off*)   Och, the roads have all changed, Sandra.

Sandra *marches thoughtlessly on to the carpet.*

Sandra   And I told the man we were in a hurry.

Enter **Rena** *with a coat on, carrying parcels, struggling a little more than* **Sandra***.*

Rena   Your father says the roads have all changed.

Sandra   And I told the man we had to get back.

Rena   Oh yes: the roads have all changed since you were last in Scotland. (Sandra!)

Sandra   Get back to receive a phone call. (What?)

She drops her parcels in the middle of the floor.

Rena   The carpet, Sandra.

Pause.

Sandra   Och, the carpet'll be dry.

She throws off her shoes and tries the carpet with her feet.

Rena   Your father's carpet.

Sandra   It is dry.

Rena   So I hope it's dry.

At the edge of the carpet, she slips off her shoes and tries the carpet with her feet.

Sandra   'Your father's carpet.'

Rena   Because I was up half of last night.

Sandra   (And what a carpet.) Oh I know you were.

Rena   Up half of last night cleaning it.

Sandra   I was up half of last night. *With* you cleaning it.

Rena   I won't bother cleaning anything else.

Sandra   Yes, don't bother cleaning anything else.

Rena/Sandra (*together*)   Just because you're visiting./ Just because I'm visiting.

Rena *is now satisfied, puts her shoes on and makes to cross the carpet to another exit.*

Rena   Oh and look. Your father hasn't left for his work yet.

Sandra   Aye, well, I wish he/

Rena   Shirt still there since I ironed it.

Sandra   I wish he/

Rena   Cup of tea lying cold. Likely.

Sandra   I wish he'd hurry up and leave for his work because/

Rena   So get this shopping junk away.

She continues towards exit. **Sandra** *crosses to pick up a chair, not picking up any bags.*

Sandra   Because I want peace, quiet and privacy to receive this phone call.

Rena   Because I don't want your father finding a mess.

Sandra *picks up a chair.*

Sandra   Well, I think my father'll let me get into the place.

Rena   You see: you don't/

Sandra *takes chair to phone and sits.*

Sandra   He'll let me put my feet up five minutes.

Rena   You don't/

Sandra   I've been out trekking round buying presents for my family from Scotland.

Rena   You don't/ Presents from Scotland for your family?

Sandra   Yes.

Rena   What about presents from America for your mother?

Sandra   I/

Rena   No, you just don't understand your father.

Sandra   Well, you shouldn't put up with my father.

Rena   I can manage your father these days.

Sandra   But you had to move into my room, didn't you?

Rena   Yes, Sandra, but/

Sandra   And it was because you couldn't stand him any more, wasn't it?

Rena   Yes, Sandra, but/

Sandra   So that's a disgrace then, isn't it? (What?)

Pause.

Rena   Things have changed since then.

Sandra   So why didn't you move back out of my old room?

Rena   What business is it of yours?

Sandra   A husband and wife – if they're together – should sleep together.

Rena   Sandra!

Sandra   Or/ What?

Rena   Who is it that's phoning you?

Sandra   No one you need bother with.

Rena   Is this you keeping secrets next?

Sandra   It's an old acquaintance from way back you won't remember.

Rena   As if I didn't have enough of that from your father, over the years.

Sandra   Has my father got secrets?

Rena   Your father's always had a secret or two on the go.

Sandra   I/

Rena   What do you think of that?

Sandra   I'm shocked and horrified, Mother. Because what I already know about my father is quiet bad enough as it is!

Rena   I/

Sandra   So what are these secrets?

Rena   I'm damned if I'm telling you.

Sandra   Why the hell not?

Rena   Because that Yankee mouth of yours is too damned big.

Sandra   I/ It is not.

Rena   I mean: the way you kept going on to that taxi driver!

Sandra   And some holiday this: insults from my father!

Rena   Did you have to keep going on to the taxi driver about American taxis?

Sandra   Insults from my mother!

Rena   'American taxis are'/

Sandra   Insults from a taxi driver!

Rena   'American taxis are'/

Sandra   Oh. Yes. And! It's 'Don't leave a mess in case of your father.'

Rena   'American taxis are'/

Sandra   Or it's 'Don't speak your mind to taxi drivers.'

Rena   'American taxi drivers are so honest.'

Sandra   Because you can't call me big mouth just because I/

Rena   I was so embarrassed.

Sandra   As a matter of principle I speak my mind to everybody.

Rena   I was so/ Oh, I know: don't remind me!

Pause.

Sandra   But you know: back home in Fraserburgh/

Rena   So stop speaking your mind about America!

Sandra   Back home in Fraserburgh, New Jersey/

Rena   Imagine 'speaking your mind' about America to your father.

Sandra   Because if I was back home in Fraserburgh, New Jersey, I'd have that vermin of a taxi driver up before the courts. (What?)

Rena   'Speaking your mind' about America's only going to put your father's back up.

Pause.

Sandra   What about my father putting my back up? 'How's the colony developing?' he goes.

Rena   And you know who has to suffer/ ?

Sandra   I'll 'colony' him. In fact, if he was in Fraserburgh, New Jersey, I'd have him up before the courts for being a dirty rotten asshole of a father.

Rena   You know who has to suffer in the long run?

Sandra   An asshole of a father and a husband!

Rena   Me!

Pause.

Sandra   Yes exactly, Mother: you!

Rena   And keep your voice down.

Sandra   So why not come back with me?

Rena   I don't want your father hearing you speak/

Sandra   Aye. Just come back with me to Fraserburgh, New Jersey.

Rena   Speaking your mind about America/ Och, I couldn't go back with you to Fraserburgh.

Sandra   You know you'd be welcome.

Rena   Imagine me in Fraserburgh.

Sandra   You know you'd be popular! So, Mother/

Rena   Fraserburgh, New Jersey. (What?)

Sandra   Promise you'll think it over.

Rena   Oh, I'll think it over.

Sandra   Good.

Rena   Aye. I'll think it over if you'll stop speaking your mind about America to your father. Because, as I say/

Sandra   I won't even mention America (What?)

Rena   It's me that's to suffer/

Sandra   Oh, I know: it's you that's to suffer/

Rena/Sandra (*together*)   In the long run.

Rena *goes to go.*

Sandra   Have a seat for a minute, Mother.

Rena   But do you/ ?

Sandra   Sit on your butt.

Rena   Do you really think I'd be popular?

Sandra   Get the coat off.

Rena   Of course, people always have said: 'It's her sense of humour has seen Rena Nauldie through.'

Sandra   Relax.

Rena   So if I ever did go to Fraserburgh, New Jersey, to live, I daresay you'd be right.

Sandra   Screw my father!

Rena   Because I daresay I would be popular. (What?)

Sandra   Screw/ In fact where is my father?

Rena   He'll be in the bath.

Sandra   Shouldn't he be going to his work?

Rena   He'll be in the bath getting ready for his work.

Sandra   I/

Rena   But do you really think I'd be popular in America?

Sandra   I/ Yes I do. Because your grandchildren and all my friends in Fraserburgh, New Jersey are dying to meet you. They're all dying to experience your sense of humour.

Rena   Oh ho ho. That's nice. And I'd like to meet my grandchildren sometime.

Sandra   I can guarantee you'll be popular and meet your grandchildren, Mother. You only have to come back with me to Fraserburgh, New Jersey, and it's all yours! So will you come?

Rena   I'd have to think it over.

Sandra   What's there to think over?

Rena   I'd hate to lose my independence.

Sandra (*insistent*)   You haven't got any independence living with my father. I mean: no one will interfere with you in America.

Rena   No one except you.

Sandra   I/

Rena   Because let's face it: you are awful dominant.

Sandra   I am not dominant. I/Aye. You wouldn't think twice about it if Patrick asked you.

Rena   Patrick?

Sandra   Yes, you wouldn't think twice if your son asked you to go to America, would you?

Rena   Don't bring up Patrick, please.

Sandra   Sorry.

Rena   Oh, forget it. It's not as if I get upset these days.

Sandra   I'll be more careful in future.

Rena   I don't get reduced to tears.

Sandra   I won't bring him up again.

Rena   I've made progress in that department. Ha ha. So I don't/

Sandra   So I won't/

Rena   I don't/

Sandra   I won't/

Rena   I don't/

Willie (*off*)   Woman!

Sandra   I/

Willie (*off*)   I say: woman!

Sandra   Well, don't you answer him.

Willie (*off*)   Heh, woman! . . . Heh, Bridget!

Sandra   Don't/ Who's Bridget?

Rena (*shouts*)   What is it?

Sandra   He's not still calling you Bridget?

Rena (*to* **Sandra**)   'Bridget' is your father's idea of a joke.

Willie (*off*)   Bring me in my clean shirt.

Sandra   Bridget!

Rena   Oh, I know!

Sandra   Your name's/

Rena   Pathetic, isn't it? (*Shouts.*) Aye, coming. (*To* **Sandra**.) 'Bridget.'

Rena *puts down her parcels and picks up shirt.*

Sandra   Well, let him get his own shirt, Mother.

Willie (*off*)   Come on, Bridget!

Rena   'Bridget.'

Willie (*off*)   And bring me in my tea.

Sandra   Let him get his shirt himself.

Rena   It's not even funny. (What?)

Sandra   And you'll take in tea over my dead body!

Rena   I/

Willie (*off*)   I'll be late for my work.

Rena (*shouts*)   Your tea'll be cold.

She tries it.

Sandra   Why can't he get it himself?

Rena (*shouts*)   It is cold.

Sandra   Why?

Rena   'Why? (Tut.) 'Why?'

Willie (*off*)   Oh, typical!

Rena   Because I don't want him running around topless.

She puts tea down.

Sandra Pardon?

Rena You seen his tits?

Sandra His tits?

Rena They're falling to bits.

Sandra Oh, Mother: ho ho.

Rena Ha ha.

Sandra Ho ho ho.

Rena Ha ha ha.

Sandra You would be so popular in Fraserburgh, New Jersey.

Rena (*shouts*) I'll make you more.

Willie (*off*) Oh, don't bother.

Rena Aye.

Willie (*off*) Not enough time, Bridget.

Rena (*shouts*) I/ (*Normal.*) 'Bridget.'

Willie (*off*) And where's this shirt, woman?

Rena (*shouts*) Coming! (*To* **Sandra**.) And put those parcels away, Sandra.

Sandra (*shouts*) I am waiting for a phone call, Mother!

Rena (*off*) What?

Sandra (*shouts*) Oh, nothing!

Sandra *goes to parcels and picks them up. She moves towards exit. The phone rings. She drops the parcels and rushes to the phone, almost knocking over a cup of tea. She catches it in time.*

Rena (*off*) Answer that phone, Sandra . . . Sandra!

Sandra *picks up the receiver.*

Sandra   Hello? . . . Oh my God, Patrick: it is you. I never thought you'd actually phone. So where are you? . . . Don't talk garbage! You can't be at the motorway. I haven't even/ . . . No! You can't come now. I haven't had time to prepare them . . . What do you mean I don't need time? I/ . . .

He has hung up. She puts phone down, muttering.

Of course I need time!

Rena *comes in without her coat.*

Sandra (*aloud*)   I need/

Rena   Have you not cleared up for me yet? . . . I asked you to clear up . . . So 'do a thing yourself', right enough.

She picks up parcels and **Sandra***'s coat. She is so heavily laden she obviously can't manage it.*

And who was that on the phone, by the way?

Sandra   I/

Rena   I see you got off the line before your old mother could overhear.

Sandra   Oh, Mother, I/

Rena *goes off as* **Willie** *comes on doing up his uniform.*

Willie (*shouting after* **Rena**)   And turn my hot water off, woman.

Rena   (*off*)   What?

Willie (*sarcastic*)   I said: 'I've had my bath now. So turn'/

Rena (*off*)   Och, I've already turned your hot-water heater off. ('My hot-water heater.')

Willie (*shouts*)   Aye, turn/ Aye, well done, Bridget.

Rena (*off*)   'Bridget.'

Willie   Your mother can be awful careless with my hot water, Sandra.

Rena (*off*)   It's not even funny.

Willie   I'm only a constable . . . So you get all you wanted?
. . . Sandra?

Sandra   Eh? Oh, is this you/ ?

Willie   All you wanted out shopping?

Sandra   Is this you on your way to work?

Willie   Because that's a surprise, isn't it?

Sandra   Is it or isn't it? (Pardon?)

Willie   Because I thought you'd have better shops in
America.

He starts looking around for cap.

Like everything else in America.

He stops looking.

You're very quiet.

Sandra   Oh/

Willie   You've usually got something to say for America.

Sandra   I/

Willie   American planes or American Scotch or/ (American
Scotch!) Or American hotels. I goes to you: 'Aye away and
stay in a hotel,' I goes: 'And good riddance.' You go: 'There's
no American hotels in Scotland.' I go: 'There's a Holiday Inn
at the airport.' You go: 'I'm not spending my holiday at the
airport.' I go: 'Aye, that's your excuse.' Ha ha. Aye very good,
Willie. 'That's your excuse.' Ha ha. You all right, Sandra?
(*Looks round vaguely.*) And if you'll take my advice you'll stop
going on about America to your mother. Otherwise your
mother will end up wanting to go to America. And you don't
want that burden round you, do you? Because your mother's
the type wouldn't know a cowboy from an Indian. Ha ha. No.
(*Looks round.*) Now, have you seen my cap anywhere?

Sandra   No. I haven't.

Willie I had it here.

Sandra I wanted to ask you something.

Willie I had it/ What is it?

Sandra It's just a wee thing.

Willie What is it?

Sandra It won't matter if/

Willie Get on with it, America.

Sandra I/ Have you heard from Patrick at all?

Willie I/

Sandra Because/

Willie Aye, I wondered when that would get brought up.

Sandra Because would you be happy to see him again?

Willie So I hope you haven't brought Patrick up to your mother either. (Happy?) Because I stopped advertising for Patrick to come home years ago. (So happy? Don't make me/) Have you brought Patrick up to your mother?

Sandra In a roundabout way, aye.

Willie Because when your mother gets upset/ Well, don't!

Sandra I/

Willie Because when your mother gets upset about Patrick, it's me that's to suffer.

Sandra But/

Willie You have to understand, Sandra, it was after Patrick left she moved into your room.

Sandra Do you blame her?

Willie And what does that mean?

Sandra Nothing! Eh, no, I just mean she was upset about Patrick. So/ Do you blame her?

Willie   Of course not. Of course she's going to be upset about her boy disappearing. What I didn't understand was: after she got over him disappearing, why didn't she move back into my room?

Sandra   Have you asked her to?

Willie   I shouldn't have to ask her. It's up to her to tell me! Of course she's going to be upset about Patrick. The kind of boy he was. He's the unnatural type, Sandra. He didn't even like fishing.

Sandra   Neither do you.

Willie   That's not the point I'm making.

Sandra   You've never even been fishing.

Willie   Yes, but if I did go I would've liked it!

Sandra   I/

Willie   No, I gave Patrick his chance, Sandra. I advertised for years. I spent a fortune advertising. I'm only a constable.

Sandra   I know. Sorry. I/

Willie   Well, it's not your fault, for once. He wasn't – I mean: I have always gone in for speaking my mind. Aye, speaking my mind to that shower of crawlers over my head. Because honesty and integrity doesn't get you promoted to sergeant these days. Oh no. It's lies and shafting your colleagues and changing your hairstyle every other week. Isn't it? Now where's my cap? (*Looks round vaguely.*) And don't bring Patrick up to your mother. Because you know what she's like.

Sandra   I know.

Willie   You know what she's like about Patrick.

Sandra   I know.

Willie   She'd cross the Atlantic on a bike for Patrick.

Sandra   Oh, I know. So what would you do if Patrick were ever to turn up?

Willie   I/ Patrick?

Sandra   Patrick.

Willie   I'd kick him out the door head first, no son of mine.

Sandra   I/

Willie   Wouldn't I? Now: my/

Sandra   Do you need your cap?

Willie   What are you talking about, America?

Sandra   Can you not just go without your cap?

Willie   I'm a professional police officer. I can't go without my/

Enter **Rena**.

Rena   Is that him going on about his cap next?

Willie   I've to go through my cases with Sergeant McIntyre.

Rena   You'll've left your cap at work likely.

Sandra   We'll look for it.

Willie   I had it here!

Sandra   Then if we find it we'll call you.

Rena   Aye, if we find it we'll bring it to you. Get to your work.

Willie   Are you two trying to get rid of me?

Rena   Oh: 'Are you two trying to get rid of me?' Of course we're trying to get rid of you.

Willie   Out of my own home too.

He goes to go.

And don't bother touching that cap. No messing about wearing it or anything. That's an official police cap, OK?

Rena   Who'd want to wear your cap?

Willie   OK?

Rena   Be all shitty wee stains likely. Splashes of blood from your poor wee criminals.

Willie   OK, I said?

Sandra   OK!

Rena   The ones you beat up in the back of your van.

Willie   Aye, I'll OK you. (What?)

Rena   I've read about people like you!

Willie   It's people like you the police force of this country protects.

Rena   I feel sorry for them.

Willie   We protect you from the criminal element. Where's your gratitude?

Rena   Take a joke, Willie. And don't worry:/

Willie   And I hope you did switch off my hot-water heater.

Rena   We won't be wearing your cap.

Willie   Bridget.

He goes to go.

Rena   'My hot-water heater.'

Willie   Well, you've never gone out and done a day's work in your life to pay for a hot-water heater, have you? Have you, Bridget? So get my cap found.

Rena   I/

Willie   And get my furniture back in here . . . Bridget. Ha ha.

Willie *goes out.*

Rena   Thanks for not getting provoked, Sandra. 'My hot-water heater.'

Sandra   So you'll definitely have to come to America now.

Rena   'My furniture.'

Sandra   You'll obviously have to get out of here.

Rena   'Bridget' when my name's Rena. (What?)

Sandra   Treatment like that is a disgrace.

Rena   Och, Sandra, that's nothing. Your father's changed for the better.

Sandra   Stop covering up for him.

Rena   Remember he used to get drunk and behave in a disgusting manner?

Sandra   Don't remind me.

Rena   Well, no longer. Oh no.

Sandra   I've still not recovered from my traumatic childhood.

Rena   Now it's a couple of Scotches and: 'Would you care to dance?'

Sandra   I've still not got over/ I don't think he's changed.

Rena   He goes: 'Put that frock thing on.'

Sandra   I saw the dirty aggression in his face.

Rena   And I'm the fly type, Sandra: I do it.

Sandra   I/

Rena   Wee dance round the coffee table, he's happy. Pathetic, isn't it?

Sandra   It is, Mother. So I think you should tell me these secrets of his.

Rena   I couldn't tell you his secrets, Sandra.

Sandra   Why not?

Rena   I know what you're like.

Sandra   What am I like?

Rena   You'd be going on about your father's hair at every opportunity.

Sandra   What about my father's hair?

Rena   Your father's actually bald.

Sandra   Well, I know that.

Rena   Who told you?

Sandra   He wears the shittiest wig I've ever seen in my life.

Rena   That wig cost £20 second-hand from a colleague.

Sandra   Exactly, Mother.

Rena   What?

Sandra   I hope his other secrets are a bit more of a secret.

Rena   OK, I'm telling you no more secrets.

Sandra   Why not?

Rena   Because that Yankee mouth of yours is too damn big.

Sandra   How can you say that about your daughter?

Rena   You'd have your father's baldness all over America.

Sandra   It's already all over America!

Rena   See what I mean?

Sandra   Which is no less than he deserves.

Rena   I/ The cap, Sandra.

Sandra   Oh, what about it?

Rena   It'll be in Patrick's old room.

Sandra   What's it doing in there?

Rena   The furniture's in there till the carpet dries. It'll be in with the furniture. Quick. Go and get it. I'll call him back.

Rena *goes out.*

Sandra (*shouts*) He'll've gone.

Rena (*off*) I don't want him back this afternoon.

Sandra You shouldn't be running after him!

Rena (*off*) Getting in my way.

Sandra I wouldn't make you run after me!

Rena (*off*) When I've to get his furniture back in. I/ He's gone.

She comes back in.

Rena We're in for it now. He'll be going: 'Watch you don't mark my good furniture.'

Sandra In America you could pop candy in your mouth day and night.

Rena 'Watch you don't scuff my carpets.'

Sandra In America you could take all the weight you'd put on off with liposuction.

Rena 'They're high-quality carpets.' (What?)

Sandra And if that didn't work either, in America you could just lay back and wear a costume-jewellery tiara!

Pause.

Rena Sandra.

Sandra Yes, Mother?

Rena I put your parcels away.

Sandra Thanks.

Rena In your room.

Sandra Yes, thanks.

Rena Beside some other parcels.

Sandra What about them?

Rena What exactly are they?

Sandra   Never you mind.

Rena   Not more presents for your family in America?

Sandra   No.

Rena (*suddenly mischievous*)   When are we getting them?

Sandra   I was going to give you them when we were all together.

Rena   We've been all together.

Sandra   The whole family.

Rena   We've been all together except for/ for/ Anyway, you shouldn't have bothered.

Sandra   It's no/

Rena   I haven't even bought you yours yet.

Sandra   It's no/ You don't need to.

Rena   You can't go back to America without a bagful of presents from your mother.

Sandra   You can't afford it.

Rena   I'll manage a wee thing.

Sandra   You don't work. In fact:/

She takes out money.

Rena   My grandchildren!

Sandra *hands money to* **Rena**.

Rena   My son-in-law. Oh no, Sandra, I/

Sandra   Take it.

Rena   Don't be aggravating.

Sandra   You're my mother.

Rena   In fact: don't be so dominant.

Sandra   You/ Sorry. You're right.

She puts money away.

Sandra   Sorry . . . So listen, Mother. I wanted to/

Rena   What's wrong with you, Sandra?

Sandra   Nothing. I just wanted to say that/

Rena   Because I hope you haven't been going on about America to your father.

Sandra   Mother!

Rena   Stirring up trouble.

Sandra   Mother!

Rena   Causing me problems. (What?)

Sandra   Patrick's coming home.

Pause.

Rena   When?

Sandra   Now.

Rena   Now?

Sandra   Right now!

Rena   Well, if I'd been warned about this/

Sandra   Patrick was the phone call.

Rena   At one time in my life, I/ (Right now?)

Sandra   Patrick was the guy on the phone. (Sorry.)

Rena   I'd've got the hoover out, the soup on and wiped the toilet.

Sandra   I should've warned you.

Rena   But Patrick?

Sandra   I kept putting it off.

Rena   Because, oh my God, Sandra: I'm not even changed.

Sandra   Oh, Patrick won't/

Rena   Look at me.

Sandra   If you want to get changed: go!

Rena   OK . . . But where's Patrick been all these/ ? And how did you/ ? I mean: oh my God, Sandra: is he all right?

Sandra   He sounds/

Rena   Does he sound well?

Sandra   He sounds/

Rena   I'm awful glad.

Sandra   So go, Mother.

Rena   OK . . . But what's he/ ? . . . And what are we/ ? . . . And Jesus Christ Almighty, Sandra: what's your father going to say?

Sandra   We'll send Patrick out if my father comes back.

Rena   We can't send Patrick out.

Sandra   We'll put him in the other room.

Rena   Will he mind?

Sandra   He won't mind, no. So sorry I didn't warn you, Mother.

Rena   Yes, but why/ ?

Sandra   I wasn't to know Patrick wouldn't leave me time to prepare you.

Rena   Why/ ?

Sandra   That's so typical of him. (What?)

Rena   Why didn't he come back before?

Sandra   Go and get changed, Mother.

She goes to go. Doorbell.

Rena   But what about your father's cap if he comes back?

Sandra   Get changed, Mother. Just get changed and have a look for the cap, OK?

Rena OK.

Rena *doesn't move.*

Sandra Mother!

Rena OK!

She goes. **Sandra** *watches her go and goes to go herself. The phone rings. She stops, then goes towards the phone. Doorbell. She stops, then goes out quickly while the phone continues to ring.*

Rena (*off*)   Sandra! . . . Answer that, will you? . . . Answer that, Sandra.

Sandra *comes back in.*

Rena (*off*)   Sandra, I said/

Sandra *picks up the receiver.*

Sandra (*to phone*)   Hello . . . She's gone to look for your cap, Dad.

Patrick *comes in carrying a bag.*

Sandra (*to phone*)   OK. See you then.

She puts phone down.

Patrick Nauldie, eh?

Patrick *nods.*

Sandra   Patrick Nauldie after all these years?

Patrick *nods.*

Sandra   Patrick Nauldie himself?

Patrick *shrugs.*

Sandra   Are you thinking of speaking?

Patrick   Sorry. I didn't expect/

Sandra   Or do I get to do all the work?

Patrick   I thought maybe/

Sandra   As usual. (What?)

Patrick   I'm surprised you're alone.

Sandra   Your mother will be through.

Patrick   I/ And where's my father?

Sandra   Why?

Patrick   I need to speak to him.

Sandra   Can you not wait?

Patrick   Actually, no. I can't.

Sandra   Well, he'll be back shortly to/

Patrick   Good.

Sandra   To/

Patrick   Perfect!

Pause.

Sandra   OK. So. The thing is: things aren't any better round here.

Patrick   Well, that doesn't surprise me.

Sandra   Things are as bad as when you left.

Patrick   Things usually don't change.

Sandra   So you left because things were bad?

Patrick   I don't remember having a reason. For leaving.

Sandra   I/

Patrick   So things are still bad?

Sandra   Yes.

Patrick   You were saying?

Sandra   Yes. Yes, they are. I/ So I want to take Mother back to America with me.

Patrick   Ah!

Sandra   He's not going to change.

Patrick   Not going to mellow, eh?

Sandra   It doesn't look like it.

Patrick   Is it a holiday you're thinking about?

Sandra   It's not a holiday she needs, Patrick, it's a life.

Patrick   Does she want to go?

Sandra   What she wants is beside the point. I'm not trekking back to America knowing he still humiliates her every day of the week.

Patrick   Does he?

Sandra   They don't even sleep together. She moved out after you left and never moved back in.

Patrick   What's wrong with that? Sounds healthy enough to me!

Sandra   Well, I think a husband and wife should sleep together.

Patrick   Even when they slept together, they didn't sleep together.

Sandra   I/ You mean . . . ?

Patrick   I do.

Sandra   Not even then?

Patrick   No!

Sandra   How do you know?

Patrick   I listened.

Sandra   You did not.

Patrick   I had to. My friends used to boast about their parents making noises. I was scared Willie and Rena were weirdos or something. But they never did make any noise. So I had to make noises up to impress my friends.

Sandra   That's even worse. It's a disgrace, that is. Married all these years and you could count their orgasms on the fingers of one hand. So definitely: you will talk to her about America?

Patrick   You want *me* to?

Sandra   She'll do anything you say. You always were the favourite.

Patrick   You were the first to get a bike.

Sandra   I was four years older!

Patrick   And you never let me have a go on it.

Sandra   I wasn't allowed to.

Patrick   I really wanted a go on it.

Sandra   I was responsible for you.

Patrick   I cried myself to sleep at night for a ride on that bike.

Sandra   I/ Och! No, it was definitely you that was the favourite! Patrick this, Patrick that.

Patrick   You're right. The more I think about it the more I realise how right you are. You didn't even know about the special messages, did you?

Sandra   What? What messages are these?

Patrick   She only ever sent me to deliver them.

Sandra   She sent me with messages too.

Patrick   These were special messages I'm talking about.

Sandra   I/ What was so special?

Patrick   Well, I don't know.

Sandra   I could've delivered them better than you.

Patrick   She didn't trust you.

Sandra   Why the hell not? I was older and more responsible.

Pause.

Patrick   You'll have to ask her about that.

Sandra   So why were they such a big deal?

Patrick   No idea.

Sandra   You mean you didn't ever open one to find out?

Patrick   Of course not.

Sandra   How could you resist?

Patrick   Maybe that explains why she didn't send you.

Sandra   I beg your pardon. I would've opened it as a matter of principle! She's got secrets, he's got secrets: what kind of family is this?

Patrick   He's got secrets?

Sandra   I've only managed to get her to tell me one. Only it wasn't a secret.

Patrick   What was it?

Sandra   She thinks I didn't know he's bald.

Patrick   Is he?

Sandra   Of course. That's all happened since you were last home. But that's not important. It's these other secrets I want to get my hands on. She's never going to tell me them. So I thought you could ask.

Patrick   Get her to go to America with you *and* the family secrets?

Sandra   That'll do nicely!

Patrick   You don't want much, do you?

Sandra   I/ Look, Patrick. I'm not having you being awkward about this.

Patrick   Oh, you're not?

Sandra   Because getting my mother to go to America is the least you can do.

Patrick   Oh, it is?

Sandra   Yes, it is! Because half the reason she's stuck it out with him is: she's been waiting for you to come back.

Patrick   I/

Sandra   And America's your mother's only escape route.

Patrick   Her only?

Sandra   Yes, it is. It's her only escape route from this/ this hell on earth.

Patrick   I/

Sandra   Oh, and what was it you wanted to say to him?

Patrick   Oh, you know. Just a few/

Sandra   We have to be careful what we say to him.

Patrick   A few old scores/

Sandra   Because we need to keep things ticking over nicely and not get up his big fat nose till the visa comes through and I can get her escorted out the country. (What?)

Patrick   I've got a few old scores to settle with him. (You know?)

Sandra   Do you think you could not bother settling any old scores?

Patrick   Oh, I must settle my scores!

Sandra   Going around settling old scores at your age.

Patrick   Oh, but settling scores with your father: that's how a boy becomes a man!

Sandra   Are you going to put settling scores above your mother's welfare?

Patrick   Never in a million years!

Sandra   I/

Pause.

Oh, and incidentally . . .

Patrick   Yes?

Sandra   How are you?

Patrick   Well. (Ha.) I could ask you the same thing.

Sandra   You could. (Ha.)

Patrick   Will I bother?

Sandra   Oh, Patrick.

Patrick   What?

Sandra   Please yourself.

Patrick   I certainly will.

Pause.

Sandra   So I meant to ask:/

Patrick   Yes?

Sandra   Are you still the musical type?

Patrick   Pardon?

Sandra   Do you still play the bagpipes?

Patrick   Well, to be quite honest, Sandra:/

Sandra   'Amazing Grace' on a Sunday morning.

Patrick   To tell you the truth:/

Sandra   Too much!

Patrick   Playing bagpipes in England would cause an international incident.

Sandra   Is that right?

Patrick   Actually, it would.

Sandra   Well, you do surprise me. Because back home in Fraserburgh, New Jersey, the bagpipes are the height of fashion!

Patrick   I/ Should I take them up again?

Sandra   I wish you would.

Patrick   Maybe I will.

Sandra   Because you were good.

Patrick   Thank you.

Pause.

Sandra   So thanks for writing to us.

Patrick   You're welcome.

Sandra   Weird, isn't it?

Patrick   It is.

Sandra   I advertised all over the world for you.

Patrick   Did you?

Sandra   And you're only over the border in England.

Patrick   I know.

Pause.

Sandra   So how long are you staying for?

Patrick   However long it takes.

Sandra   However long what takes?

Patrick   Whatever it is I'm doing.

Sandra   What are *you* up to?

Patrick   What are you up to?

Sandra   I think we know what I'm up to.

Pause.

Patrick   What about your family?

Sandra   What about them?

Patrick   Why didn't you bring them?

Sandra   Well, it's nice to get a rest from being a wife and mother.

Patrick   There's nothing wrong though?

Sandra   Why should there be? Oh no. They're the best little family in the whole wide world.

Patrick   I/

Sandra   And also, Patrick, I thought if I bring the boys she'll get to see them again and be less tempted to come back with me. And you're all right about that, aren't you?

Patrick   Well am I?

Sandra   Well are you?

Patrick   Whatever.

Pause.

Sandra   So what's it like in England?

Patrick   It?

Sandra   Yes. It. In fact: what are taxi drivers like in England?

Patrick   Taxi drivers?

Sandra   Because round here they're a thieving lot of/

Patrick   They're the same all over!

Sandra   A thieving lot of/ I beg your pardon! American taxi drivers are the kind of people you invite into your house!

Patrick   Which you do whenever you want a rest from being a good wife and mother.

Pause.

Sandra   You know, Patrick, you've changed.

Patrick   In what way?

Sandra   I don't know. You just seem really, really/ I can't put my finger on it.

Patrick   Don't worry.

Sandra   I won't.

Patrick   It'll come to you.

Sandra   Of course, you always were a right pain in the butt.

Patrick   How interesting.

Sandra   What?

Patrick   How interesting you make me sound!

Sandra   *What?*

Patrick   Whatever.

Pause.

Rena *comes in.*

Rena   Where have you been, Patrick Nauldie?

Patrick   Mother!

Rena   I must have been round that block a good thirty or forty times looking for you in the last ten years. People are beginning to notice!

Patrick   I/

Rena   You might have left a note to say you'd popped out. Your father paid a fortune for adverts.

Patrick   I'm really/

Rena   And he took every penny out of my housekeeping! (What?)

Patrick   I'm sorry, Mother.

Rena   I don't want you to feel bad for ruining my life, Patrick.

Patrick   What do you want?

Rena   Oh, just what any mother would want at a time like this, son. To get the arrangements sorted out. How long are you staying?

Patrick   As long as it takes.

Rena   Half an hour probably.

Patrick   We'll need to see!

Rena   I thought so: 'We'll need to see.' He hasn't changed. Has he, Sandra?

Sandra   I/

Rena   He's still a pain in the neck! . . . Have you got nothing to say for yourself, Patrick?

Patrick   I/

Rena   That's pathetic. I haven't seen you since the last time I saw you.

Patrick   Mother, I/

Rena   The least you could do is say something.

Patrick   I/

Rena   How do I look, Sandra?

Sandra   I/

Patrick   You look very nice, Mother.

Rena   Your father bought my dress.

Sandra   How did he scrape the money together? He's only a constable!

Rena   He got some/

Patrick   Still a constable?

Rena   He got some football duty overtime last winter.

Patrick   (Fuck.)

Sandra   Of course he's still a constable.

Rena   Patrick!

Sandra   He should be getting kicked out, never mind promoted!

Rena   Sandra! Well, neither of you have changed. Fully grown adults the pair of you. Fully grown adults and still cheeky.

Sandra/Patrick   Sorry, Mother.

Rena *sheds a silent tear.*

Patrick   So where's this father of mine?

Sandra   He's going to call round and collect his/ (*To* **Rena**.) Did you find his cap, Mother. Mother? What is it?

Rena   Oh/ I/ I haven't looked for his cap yet!

Sandra   That's all right then. But what is it?

Rena   Nothing!

Sandra   OK! I was only trying to/

Another sob from **Rena**.

Patrick (*to* **Sandra**)   What's wrong with her?

Sandra (*to* **Rena**)   What's wrong with you?

Rena   It's just that/ That's the first time you two have been cheeky since I told you off for coming back late from the ice rink.

Sandra   I wasn't cheeky.

Rena   You were cheeky! Cheeky as/

Sanddra   Was I? Was I cheeky?

Rena   You said I was an old square.

They all laugh together.

Patrick   I'm glad you're so well, Mother.

Rena   Och aye, son. I'm not bad.

Sandra   Listen to her.

Rena   I struggle by.

Sandra   When I think I have just witnessed one of the most shocking humiliations!

Rena   No, no, son. My situation is definitely improving.

Sandra   And all over some hot water for a bath!

Rena   Your father doesn't approve of waste!

Sandra   It was a shocking, humiliating incident!

Rena   I/

Sandra   It would never happen in America!

Pause.

Rena   Your sister doesn't half go on about America, Patrick.

Sandra   That's because in America/

Rena   In America everyone's perfect.

Sandra   Because in America/

Rena   In America everyone's beautiful.

Sandra   Aye. At least in America no one is mean with their hot water.

Rena   Aye. In America everyone's mean with their hot shite.

Sandra   I/

Rena   See what you've got me saying, Sandra?

Sandra   I'm sorry, I suppose.

Rena   You never hear language from me normally!

Sandra   I said I'm sorry.

Rena   That's all right. Now, Patrick/

Sandra   Yes, but/

Rena   Well, Patrick/

Sandra   So, Mother/

Rena   I can deal with your father nowadays.

Sandra   Yes but his cap, Mother.

Rena   Take this afternoon/

Patrick   I/

Sandra   I'll go and get it.

Rena   Take this afternoon, Patrick/

Patrick   His cap?

Sandra   I/ Yes, his cap!

Rena   This afternoon I said to Willie:/

Patrick   Does he still have to wear a cap?

Rena   Of course, son./ Every day.

Patrick   I remember his cap.

Rena   I/

Patrick   I used to say: 'Daddy, let me wear your cap.' He'd go: 'Away and play.' Ha ha.

Rena   Ha ha. Aye, you wore his cap all right. You stole his cap while he wasn't looking, stuck it on your head till it came halfway down your face and said: 'Mummy, can I have an increase in my pocket money?' Ha ha.

Patrick   Ha ha. And I never got that increase, did I?

Rena   Neither you did, son. Because we were poor people.

Patrick   So I think it's about time I got that cap on and tried again, don't you?

Rena   Oh, don't wear his cap, son. He'll/

Sandra   What are you talking about wearing his cap for?

Rena   He won't see the joke!

Sandra   Imagine you in his cap and him around!

Patrick   I/

Sandra   It's just not funny!

Rena   So promise your mother you won't ever wear his cap, son.

Patrick   I don't know if I can promise that, Mum.

Sandra   Listen to it. Why the hell not?

Rena   Yes, why not, son?

Patrick   I want to wear his cap because/ Because it's against the rules for people like me to wear his cap.

Rena   What do you mean?

Sandra   'People like you'? What kind of person are you?

Patrick   You really want to know?

Sandra   What?

Rena   Yes, what kind of person are you, Patrick?

Patrick   I'm a criminal.

Pause.

Rena   Oh, Patrick/

Sandra   How can you/ ?

Rena   You're terrible. Ha ha.

Patrick   Ha ha.

Rena   I see you've developed a sense of humour too, son. Ha ha.

Patrick   Ha ha. The only thing is, Mother: it's not actually a joke. I *am* a criminal.

Pause.

Rena   I'll just go out and make your tea, son.

Sandra   No. I'll make the tea.

Rena   No, Sandra, I'll/ (*To* **Patrick**.) And is there anything you want with it? A cake?

Patrick   Oh. Ah yes, actually, Mum/

Rena   A biscuit?

Patrick   I'd kill for a hot bath.

Pause.

Rena   Of course, son.

Sandra   And what do you want a hot bath for?

Patrick   I/

Rena   Of course, son. I'll put the hot water back on.

Sandra   No, I'll put it/ Well, my father won't like that.

Rena   Garbage, Sandra.

Sandra   Wasting hot water! (*To* **Patrick**.) This is not you settling scores again, is it?

Rena   I'll sort your father out.

Sandra   Is it, Patrick?

Patrick   Thanks, Mum. That's good of her to sort my father out. Isn't it, Sandra? (What?)

Sandra   Is it?

Patrick   Whatever.

Sandra *goes to go.*

Rena   Where are you going, Sandra Michigan?

Sandra   Mother.

Rena   What?

Sandra   I'll make the tea. I'll put the hot-water heater on. In fact: I'll find the cap.

Rena   Are you sure you can manage?

Sandra   I/ You entertain Patrick with your sense of humour.

Rena   Are you sure you can/ ? Oh yes ha ha. My sense of humour!

Sandra   And Patrick's got a lot to say to you before his bath. Haven't you, Patrick?

Patrick   I/

Sandra *cuts across him going to exit and knocks over the tea which spills on the carpet.*

Rena   Och, Sandra.

Sandra   It was an accident.

Rena   You've stained your father's carpet.

Sandra   Who cares?

Rena   Well, you know what he's like about his carpet.

Sandra   I know. And he shouldn't be like what he's like about his carpet.

Rena   He's like what he's like!

Sandra   And I'll clean it up.

Rena   I/ No, Sandra

Sandra   I'm . . . cleaning . . . it . . . up, Mother.

Sandra *goes to go.*

Rena   Oh, you're wasting your time cleaning it up, Sandra. You've stained it.

Sandra   I'll get it out somehow.

Rena   Och, Sandra, you've had no experience of pale blue carpets.

Sandra   Yes, exactly, Mother.

Rena   I/

Sandra   Because you don't get stupid-looking pale blue carpets in America.

Sandra *goes out.* **Rena** *goes to investigate the stain.*

Rena   And between you and me, Patrick: I think Sandra's missing her family. Because she's been a hellish moody bitch since she arrived from America. And she'll never get that lifted. It's tea, Patrick. It stains. And I don't know who she takes it from. Oh – ha – unless she takes her moods from her father.

Patrick   Ha. How is he?

Rena   Oh, same as usual, son.

Patrick   Same habits?

Rena   Not quite as bad. The temper's died down.

Patrick   Good.

Rena   Increase in my housekeeping.

Patrick   Progress.

Rena   And the girlfriend's out the window.

Patrick   That's really/ What did you say?

Rena   He doesn't have a girlfriend any more, Patrick.

Patrick   When did he have a girlfriend?

Rena   Och, son. I can't remember.

Patrick   How did you find out?

Rena   He used to come home late. He said he was working. I didn't believe him. So I followed him one afternoon. And he went to a flat.

Patrick   How do you know that was his girlfriend?

Rena   I followed him a few times.

Patrick   How many times?

Rena   Twenty-seven.

Patrick   I/

Rena   And when I didn't follow him he was still that bit late.

Patrick   Is it still going on?

Rena   Oh no. It stopped a few months after it began.

Patrick   How do you know?

Rena   That's enough secrets for now, Patrick.

Sandra *comes in with a cloth and starts work.*

Rena   Ha ha. She's wasting her time, Patrick. You're wasting your time, Sandra. And there's some spare/

Sandra   It won't move.

Rena   There's/ I said that to you.

Sandra   I/ Right, Mother. And if my father kicks up a stink about a wee tea stain all over his stupid-looking pale blue carpet I'll split his skull open.

Rena   Sandra.

Sandra   Yes, Mother?

Rena   Bring me the stanley knife from under the sink.

Sandra   What for?

Rena   Just bring it, Sandra.

Sandra *goes out.*

Rena   Well, Patrick, I suppose you'll have to tell me what you've been doing with yourself.

Patrick   I/

Rena   While your old mother was traipsing round the back streets hunting for you.

Patrick   Well, Mother: I/

Rena   Probably a catalogue of enjoyments!

Patrick   I, eh/ Me?

Rena   You! (If I know you.) Probably too busy enjoying yourself to even think about your old mother. Aye! But I'll get the whole sordid story out of you some day. Ha.

Patrick   Ha.

Sandra *comes in with knife and hands it to* **Rena**. **Rena** *goes over and cuts off the area where the stain is, expanding the area of floor showing. She gives the cut carpet to* **Sandra**, *who goes out.*

Rena   What is wrong with her? Do you know she's been trying to dominate me by getting me to go to America. As if I'd go there. Sitting round in the lap of luxury all day. Getting dominated by Sandra. Mind you. There's big Ronnie. Lovely tan. Always a nice tie with a lovely shirt. I could just fancy the hunk. But your sister'll have him like that. (*Gestures.*) Ha ha.

Patrick   Ha ha.

Rena   Ha ha. But I'm awful glad to see you again. How are you, son?

Patrick   Oh/

Rena   Well, that'll all have to wait for now. Your father's due back.

Patrick   I want to say something to you, Mother. While we're alone. I don't want you to be in any doubt why I stayed away so long. The reason is I was scared I'd hit my father.

Rena   Oh, Patrick/

Patrick   Yes! And I had the idea that if I stayed away long enough I wouldn't want to hit him any more. Well, I waited and waited, but the feeling that I wanted to hit my father just wouldn't go away. I thought I might never be able to go home and see my mother again. But then I saw Sandra's advert. 'Patrick Nauldie come home.' And I realised that there never would come a time when I wouldn't want to hit my father. So if I wanted to see my mother again I'd just have to go home anyway and risk it. So let's just see if I can be in the same room as my father and control my desire to hit him.

Rena   I don't know what you're worried about, Patrick. I've never lost the desire to hit your father. Ha ha.

Patrick   Ha ha.

Rena   Ha ha. That's quite a sense of humour you've been developing. Just like your old mother's. And I hope you didn't come just for your father, Patrick Nauldie. Just to hit or not hit your father.

Patrick Oh no, Mother. I've also got ideas for you.

Rena Surely not.

Patrick So, you were saying there's no chance of you going to America?

Rena Well, there's not no chance. Apparently if I went to Fraserburgh, New Jersey, to live I'd be very popular. Big Ronnie. Chocolates. Jewellery. Grandchildren. The list is endless. If I could just get rid of Sandra somehow. I never trusted that daughter of mine, Patrick. That's why it was you I sent to deliver my special messages. And you always delivered them safely, son, didn't you?

Patrick Would it have been bad if I haven't delivered them, Mum?

Rena Very bad. That's why I know you delivered them, son.

Patrick What do you mean?

Rena Nothing bad ever happened to me. So I don't think I'll bother with America.

Patrick No?

Rena No. You proud of me?

Patrick Very. You've moved on from the old Rena, Mum. You'll take shit from no one. I remember you when you were a timid wee thing. I took you to the jobcentre to encourage you to be more independent and get a job?

Rena How could I forget? That was the last place I saw you.

Patrick I know. And I'm sorry. It was just when you refused to go for that cleaning job at the sewage works I felt that was the last straw, you know? The world was closing in on me and I had to get out. So I did.

Rena You just walked out and left me! But we won't rake all that up, son. Now. What's this idea you've got for your mother? Because I really will have to get my life sorted out.

Patrick   Good. So. How would you like to get away from Willie?

Rena   For how long?

Patrick   As long as you like.

Rena   For good?

Patrick   For as long as you like.

Rena   How would I live, Patrick?

Patrick   Maybe we could find a way.

Rena   You don't mean move in with you?

Patrick   I/

Rena   Because try as I might, I would just cramp your style if I moved in with you. You'd be wanting to enjoy yourself all the time and I/

Patrick   You couldn't move in with me.

Rena   I/ Why's that, Patrick?

Patrick   Because I'm a criminal.

Rena   You/ Now I don't know why you keep going on about criminals, Patrick.

Patrick   I told you, Mother. I am one.

Rena   Well, I can't work out why you keep repeating yourself. Because the first rule of a sense of humour is not to hammer a joke to death. But thanks very much for the offer of buying me a house.

Patrick   What?

Rena   I will think it over.

Patrick   That's not what I/

Car horn is tooted.

Sandra (*off*)   Oh my God . . . He's here.

Rena   I will/ That's him here. What are we going to do? I/

Sandra *comes in.*

Sandra   Right, Patrick. Out.

Patrick   What?

Sandra   Till we get time to prepare him.

Patrick   I/

Sandra   We'll need time to prepare him, Mother, won't we?

Rena   Oh yes, son. I/

Rena *discovers knife in her hand. She gives it to* **Patrick**. *He puts it in his bag and goes.*

Sandra   Right, Mother. I'll get the cap and we can send my father away.

Rena   You/ What about Patrick?

Sandra   We're sending my father away.

Rena   Patrick wants to talk to him.

Sandra   He'll be wanting to settle old scores, Mother.

Rena   Will he?

Sandra   And we're not risking trouble, are we?

Rena   No. I know what you mean. Patrick will tell your father he's a criminal.

Sandra   I/

Rena   And Willie won't get the joke. But what will we tell Patrick?

Sandra   We'll tell Patrick he was in a hurry.

Rena   In a hurry?

Sandra   In a hurry, Mother, to get back to his/

Rena   Aye. In a hurry to get back out and arrest more criminals.

Sandra *goes to go, but is stopped when* **Willie** *comes in.*

Willie   Where's my cap?

Rena   I/

Sandra   I was just on my way to/

Willie   Have you not found it yet?

Sandra   To/

Willie   Have you pair been at it?

Rena   I/ I'll go and/

Sandra   I'll go and get it.

Willie   No.

Rena   It's no/

Willie   I'm in a hurry.

Sandra   It's/

Willie   I've a colleague out there waiting.

Rena   I/

Willie   I'll get it myself.

He goes to go and thinks better of it.

Because I don't want any of you pair dancing round wearing it.

Sandra   I don't/

Rena   We wouldn't be wearing it.

Willie   You/ Och!

He goes to go.

Rena   So watch what you're saying, boy. 'Wearing your cap.' More of that and I'll take my independence back.

Sandra *finds this significant.*

Willie   You?

Sandra   Her!

Rena   Any more and I'll leave.

Willie   You?

Sandra   Her!

Rena   Then who'd iron your shirts?

Willie   And where would you go? 'Shirts.'

Rena   I've got a variety of options available to me.

Willie   Och/

Rena   So watch your lip.

Willie   My lip? Ha. Aye, very good, Bridget. My lip. Ha ha. My/ ? Heh, wait a minute. (*To* **Sandra**.) Is this your work, America?

Sandra   Me? I/

Willie   This 'variety of options'?

Sandra   Oh, it's always me, isn't it?

Willie   More of that and you can go and stay in one of your American hotels.

Sandra   I/ Well, I *might just* go and stay in a/

Rena   Don't bother with him, Sandra.

Sandra   I'm going to a hotel.

Rena   He's a poor tormented wreck of a lonely person.

Willie   Lonely? Away and/

Sandra   I'm an employee of the Holiday Inn in Fraserburgh, New Jersey.

Rena   So don't listen to him.

Willie   Away and don't talk shite, woman.

Rena   You can't afford a hotel, Sandra.

Sandra   So if I went to the Holiday Inn/

Willie   I have got friends like/

Rena   Friends? Hah! Don't make me/

Willie   Aye! Friends: I'm up to my/

Rena   Don't make me/ Aye. Friends coming out your arse/!
. . . (What?)

Sandra   So if I went to the Holiday Inn at the airport I'd be
entitled to a discount.

Willie *goes to go.*

Rena   Where did you say this cap was?

Willie   You know where it is.

Rena   Remind me again.

Willie   In Patrick's/

Rena (*extra loud voice*)   In Patrick's room?

Willie   Aye. And out my way you foul-mouthed trollop.

Rena (*extra loud voice*)   What's it doing in Patrick's room?

Willie   You put it there when you cleaned my carpets in a
disorganised fashion . . . Bridget.

He goes to go.

Rena   'Bridget.'

Patrick *comes in, still carrying his bag and carrying the cap.*

Patrick   Hello, Dad. Long time no see. Is this it?

Patrick *seems to offer the cap to* **Willie. Willie** *does not respond.*
Patrick *withdraws cap.*

Rena   Surprise! Surprise! (Ha ha.)

Patrick   This is it, isn't it?

Willie   Right. OK:/

Sandra   Dad, we/

Willie   OK now:/

Rena   Willie, we/

Willie   No explanations!

Pause.

Rena   I/

Sandra   We/

Willie   No explanations, I said. The cap.

Patrick   So it is your cap!

Willie   The cap!

Patrick   I'd hate to think I'd made a mistake!

Willie   The cap, I said.

Patrick   Because I'd hate to think I'd been wearing someone else's cap. And that/

Willie   Wear my cap?

Patrick   And/

Willie   You?

Patrick   And, I said, that I'd been wearing your cap for nothing.

Pause.

Rena   Oh, Pat/

Willie   OK/

Rena   Patrick, son/

Willie   OK/

Rena   You can't wear your father's cap.

Willie   Just hand it/

Patrick   Oh, ah sorry, I/

Willie   Hand it over! (What?)

Patrick   I can't. (Sorry.)

Pause.

Sandra   Look Patrick: don't mess about.

Patrick   Ah/

Sandra   My dad's to get back to his work.

Patrick   Oh/

Sandra   There's a policeman waiting outside.

Patrick   Sorry, Sandra.

Rena   Patrick, son. Give your father his cap. I/

Patrick   No! . . . Sorry, Mother.

Pause.

Rena   How are you enjoying the surprise, Willie?

Willie   Right, no more!

Patrick   Oh, Daddy/

Willie   No more, I said. And don't 'Daddy' me. The/

Patrick   I'm disappointed you're not curious about me, Daddy.

Willie   The cap!

Patrick   I'm very curious about you, Daddy.

Willie   You/ ? (*To* **Rena** *and* **Sandra**.) What/ ? . . . What's been/ ?

Rena   Oh/

Sandra   Ah/

Patrick   But I can't give you your cap, Dad.

Willie   You/ ?

Patrick   I haven't had my hot bath yet . . . Have I, Mum?

Rena   Oh, Pat/

Patrick   Have I, Sandra?

Sandra   You/

Patrick   And the bathroom's the only place I'll get to wear your cap without someone trying to swipe it off me, isn't it?

Willie   Right!

Rena   Oh, Sandra/

Willie   That's it.

Sandra   What, Mother?

Willie   Because no bath. Because no/

Rena   What happened/ ?

Willie   No hot water of mine.

Rena   What happened to that cup of tea, Sandra?

Willie   And shut the mouth, you pair. I'm talking. Now/

Patrick   Oh, Dad/

Willie   And/

Patrick   You/

Willie   You won't be wearing my cap!

Patrick   You'll never talk like that to my mother and sister again, OK?

Willie   Jesus Christ, boy: what is this? I/ I've got my work to go to. I've never been/ I've never had a day off work in my/ So just give me the/

Patrick   Never?

Rena   Give your dad his/

Willie   Never!

Patrick   Well, there is always a first for everything. (Sorry, Mum.)

Willie   This is all a load of/ If you don't give me my/ I'll/ I'll/

Patrick   I don't think so.

Willie   I/ What?

Patrick   I don't think you'll whatever ever again.

Willie   Right, you two. (*To* **Rena** *and* **Sandra**.) What's happened to/ ? Well, do you know what's happened to my son?

Rena   Oh, Willie, it's just a/

Patrick   Son? Son, is it? I'm his 'son'?

Rena   I think it's just a joke.

Patrick   Because use words like 'son', Dad, and/

Rena   Isn't it, Patrick?

Patrick   And you might upset me. I don't know if it's a joke, Mother. Ask Dad if he's joking. Are you joking, Dad?

Willie   Look, Patrick, can we/ ? Can you just give me my cap?

Patrick   Sorry, but no. Sorry, because you've got too much to answer for.

Willie   Eh?

Patrick   Haven't you?

Willie   Och, away, you, and/

Patrick   And you'll answer for it right after my hot bath.

Willie   Away/ Heh: I said/ (*To* **Rena** *and* **Sandra**.) You two: when I go back to work, no hot bath for him, OK? OK?

Patrick   So many terrible crimes to answer for.

Sandra   I/ What?

Patrick   Hasn't he, Mum?

Sandra   What do you mean, Patrick?

Patrick   Hasn't he, Sandra?

Sandra   Because I had a much worse childhood than you.

Pause.

Rena   Sandra Nauldie/

Sandra   Because the fights were much more violent before you were born.

Rena   Don't you dare talk like that about your childhood.

Sandra   And the foul language a lot more offensive.

Rena   You're too cheeky! When I think of what I have suffered for/

Willie   Suffered?

Rena   Suffered for you, Sandra Nauldie.

Sandra   I didn't ask to be brought into the world.

Rena   Suffered for you. From him. (What?)

Sandra   And until I met Ronnie, it wasn't worth being brought into.

Willie   What's going on?

Rena   Oh wasn't it?

Willie   You selfish load of/

Rena   And you, you big violent pig you. I/

Willie   Selfish load of swine.

Rena   I/

Willie   When I think what it was like to be a constable on the streets of/ of/ I waded through razor gangs on a daily basis.

Rena I/

Willie Daily: just to keep you all in luxuries.

Pause. Horn is tooted.

Rena Oh. Right, Patrick son.

Willie Yes. Enough.

Rena Give your father his cap now.

Willie The cap.

Rena The joke's over.

Willie My colleague is waiting. He's/

Patrick I don't think you've understood me, Dad. So if you'd like to send your colleague away, I'll explain.

Willie I/ What? What?

Patrick Just send your colleague away. Because you're not going back to work. Ever. Are you?

Pause.

Rena Ha ha.

Willie OK/

Rena Anyone feel like tea yet?

Patrick Oh, not for/

Willie OK/

Patrick Not for me. You, Dad?

Willie I/ You/ Tea? Wait a minute. (*To* **Sandra**.) What were you saying to me earlier? Because have you got something to do with him coming here? Aye, coming here without my consent?

Sandra I/ You/ Don't you/

Patrick Stop! Stop right now. Because I think I can set you all right here.

Willie Oh? Oh, that's good!

Rena Aye, good, Patrick: tell him, son.

Willie I/ What? Tell me what?

Patrick Well, there's nothing macabre or underhand about my presence here today, Dad. Oh no. Because, in a way, everybody, I've come home to celebrate.

Pause.

Sandra Look, Patrick. I know we've all got a lot to complain about. It's a tough old life. I know that. But is it really/ ?

Patrick Sandra, I/

Sandra Is it really worth all this?

Patrick All what, Sandra? Don't/

Sandra Because we'll all be getting away from here, soon. Won't we? So why don't you give my dad his/ ?

Rena Oh, I know. We're all leaving. So/

Sandra His/

Willie Oh, 'leaving'? And where might you be going, Bridget?

Rena I'm/ ('Bridget.' Tut.)

Willie You couldn't leave.

Willie *laughs.*

Sandra What do you mean, Mother? (*To* **Patrick**.) Because I thought she/ (*To* **Rena**.) I thought you had/ (*To* **Patrick**.) I thought she was coming to America. With me.

Rena Me?

Willie Aye, take her to America.

Rena Where did you get that idea?

Sandra Patrick! What's/ ?

Willie   Take her to the colony. Ha ha.

Patrick   Ha ha. Sorry, Sandra. Mum just doesn't seem to want to go to America. Isn't that right, Mum?

Rena   Oh yes, Patrick.

Patrick   I/

Sandra   If she isn't coming to America with me/

Rena   Because Patrick's/

Sandra   Where is she going?

Rena   Patrick's getting his old mother a house.

Willie *and* **Sandra** *laugh.*

Rena   Why are you laughing?

Patrick   Yes, why?

Rena   Don't you laugh at me.

Patrick   For all you know.

Rena   So why are you laughing?

Sandra   Because things like this just don't happen in Fraserburgh, New Jersey.

Patrick   Not in the bagpipe town, eh?

Willie   Fraserburgh/ ? The/ ? Ha ha. Aye, very good, Patrick. 'The bagpipe town.' Ha ha.

Patrick   Ha ha.

Sandra   You/

Horn is tooted.

Willie   Right. That's him now. So. The/

Patrick   You see. There you go again!

Rena   Oh, do without your cap. This once.

Willie   I/

Rena   Save a lot of bother.

Patrick   Trouble understanding me.

Willie   I'll trouble you.

Willie *tries to take the cap.* **Patrick** *dodges.* **Willie***'s wig loosens.*

Rena   Oh, Patrick/

Patrick   Uh-uh.

Rena   Patrick, son/

Patrick   Don't try that again.

Rena   Yes. Because I think Patrick means it, Willie.

Willie *and* **Patrick** *stand apart.*

Sandra   Right, Patrick Nauldie: why did you come here?

Patrick   Do you really want to know?

Sandra   Because did you come here to cause trouble?

Patrick   I've come home to tell you all something very important.

Rena   Aye, Patrick, tell him. It'll be about my house, won't it, son?

Patrick   No, Mum.

Rena   What's it about then?

Patrick   I've written a book.

Pause.

Willie   I don't believe it. Or/

Rena   That's why he's been too busy to write to his mother.

Willie   Or if there is a book it'll be drivel!

Sandra   That's why he's been acting like a maniac.

Willie   Only decent people write books.

Horn is tooted impatiently.

Sandra   Will I go out and speak to that cop, Dad?

Willie   And you never were the educated type, by the way. Leaves school at sixteen. Runs away from home at eighteen.

Sandra   Will I go out and send him off?

Willie   Who'd publish you?

Sandra   That's why he didn't want you to go to work, Dad.

Willie   Who'd/ ? The cap.

Sandra   He wanted you to stay home and celebrate. Congratulations, Patrick. Could I have a signed copy? They'll love that in Fraserburgh, New/

Horn is tooted impatiently.

He's obviously getting impatient, Dad.

Willie   Impatient? (You're going nowhere, America.) I'll impatient him. He'll not be impatient with me. He can wait. He'll wait till I'm ready. These young cops. I'm ashamed of them, so I am. Enforcing the laws of this country: unshaven, the trousers not pressed, and the hair all dyed to buggery. I/ And that one out there's *got a degree.*

Pause.

I'm out of here. And if you/

Patrick   You don't seem happy for me, Dad.

Willie   If you so much as/ as/ as/ If you start messing about with my cap and in any way whatsoever do damage to it I'll/ I'll/ Happy? I/

Rena   Don't bother with him, Patrick. *We're* happy for you.

Patrick   Thanks, Mum. But you know a boy likes to please his father.

Willie   Hah.

Willie *goes to go.*

Patrick   No!

Patrick *blocks his way.*

Sandra   Just let him go, Patrick.

Patrick   He's going nowhere. Because where would I be today without my father? Without my father what would I have written about? Yes, what would I have written about if he hadn't done so many atrocious things to us all?

Willie   I/

Rena   I hope you've not been writing about your father, Patrick. Who'd be interested in him?

Willie   Who'd be interested in what he writes?

Sandra   I would.

Willie   He didn't even like fishing.

Sandra   I would.

Willie   He'd go: 'What use is fishing?' Well, it's more use than some book!

Sandra   They love writers in America!

Willie   The cap! Or I'll/

Rena   Oh, Patrick. He's going to have you arrested!

Patrick   I don't mind being arrested, Mother. I'm used to it. I'm a criminal.

Willie   I/

Pause.

Rena   I'll have to get a start on getting that furniture back in, Willie.

Willie   I/

Sandra   I don't care what you say. I'm going to see your colleague. I mean: poor guy.

Willie   You/

Patrick   Yes and I'll nip up and have my bath now, Dad.

Yes, I'll just go and lock myself in the bathroom and have a damn good wear of your cap. Before you have me arrested.

As **Patrick** *goes to go,* **Willie** *lunges to get the cap.* **Sandra** *tries to intervene. The way it works out* **Willie**'s *clenched fist ends up close to* **Sandra**'s *face.* **Patrick** *moves in to protect* **Sandra** *and ends up with his fist close up to* **Willie**'s *face. At which point* **Willie**'s *wig slides slowly down his face to be caught by* **Patrick**. **Patrick** *tries to give it back to* **Willie**. **Willie** *snatches it.* **Willie** *withdraws from* **Sandra**. **Patrick** *withdraws from* **Willie**. **Willie** *slowly collapses into a chair, holding the wig and is ignored.*

Patrick   I controlled it, Mother. Are you proud of me?

Rena *bursts into tears.*

Sandra   What is it now, Mother?

Patrick   What's wrong?

Rena   I'm just so pleased my son's turned out a success.

Sandra   I/

Horn is tooted. **Sandra** *goes out.*

Patrick   Thanks, Mum. I owe all my success to the family. So let's celebrate. Let's open the presents.

Rena   Oh Patrick. Have you bought your mother a present?

Patrick   No, Mum.

Rena   Thanks very/ No?

Patrick   Sorry.

Rena   Well, you might have bought your old mother a present after all these/

Patrick   But Sandra did.

Rena   After all these years you didn't/ ? (What?)

Patrick   Sandra bought us all a present.

He goes into his bag and produces three presents. He gives one each to **Willie** *and* **Rena** *and keeps the other.* **Willie** *holds his absently.*

Rena   What about Sandra?

Patrick   Who cares about Sandra?

Rena   Yes, who cares about Sandra?

Patrick   Who cares about anyone?

Patrick *rips open his present with exaggerated gaeity. He finds a set of bagpipes in a weird pastel check that is clearly not tartan. Encouraged by this,* **Rena** *starts unwrapping as* **Sandra** *comes in.*

Sandra   Patrick Nauldie!

Patrick   Hi, Sandra! Are you back?

Sandra   I/

Rena   Thanks for the present, Sandra.

Sandra   Mum, Dad. Don't open yours.

She goes to grab them. Then thinks better of it.

Have you been in my room, Patrick Nauldie?

Patrick   Of course, Sandra. I always go into people's rooms. I'm a criminal.

Sandra *fumbles trying to reclose* **Rena**'s *present. Gives up and bursts into tears.*

Rena   What are you crying for, Sandra?

Sandra   I/

Rena   Patrick's not really a criminal. It's just his sense of humour!

Sandra   I wanted to give them out when I had you all together.

Patrick   We're all together now.

Sandra   Oh, forget it.

Patrick   Aren't we?

Sandra   It's too late.

Patrick   And I think they're great.

Sandra   The surprise is spoilt. (What?)

Patrick   They're great. Thanks.

Sandra   Oh – ha – it's nothing.

Patrick   No, really. They're wonderful. What are they?

Sandra   It's/ They're bagpipes, of course.

Patrick   They're not tartan.

Sandra   They are tartan. That is tartan. It's American tartan. It's Fraserburgh, New Jersey, tartan. They're American Bagpipes.

Patrick   I'm sorry for spoiling your surprise.

Sandra   Oh ho ho. That's all right.

Rena   Can we open ours now?

Sandra   Oh/

Willie   American tartan. Ho ho. American bagpipes. Ha ha.

Patrick   I'm going for my bath. What are you doing, Willie?

Willie   Sergeant McIntyre. Sorry I was held up, but/

Patrick   Willie?

Willie   My son's a criminal. Ha ha.

Patrick   Ha ha.

Willie   Ha ha.

Patrick *puts the cap on,* **Willie** *goes to reach for it.* **Patrick** *effortlessly forces him back down and, producing a manuscript from his bag, gives it to* **Willie** *and goes out.* **Rena** *is busy unwrapping.*

Sandra   He's turned out a really amazing guy, our Patrick.

Willie   I provide for a household.

Sandra   Hasn't he, Mum?

Willie   I protect the population.

Sandra   All the way from England to see us.

Willie   I train up the young.

Sandra   And all he can think about's a bath! Ha ha.

Willie *suddenly gets up.*

Willie   To get kicked in the teeth. Kicked in the teeth. Kicked in the/

He chants as he goes out. **Rena** *discovers a skirt in the same material as the bagpipes. And matching framed photographs of her grandchildren and Ronnie.*

Rena   Oh, Sandra, they're my grandchildren! They're:/

Willie (*off*)   Where is he?

Rena   They're/ Patrick's in the bath, Willie.

Willie (*off*)   Because wait till I get hold of him.

Enter **Willie**. **Rena** *puts the present to one side and starts to unwrap* **Willie***'s present.*

Willie   These young cops! I'll have him/

Sandra   He'd had an emergency call.

Willie   My consent is required!

Sandra   He'll call back for you later.

Willie   I'll have the punk rocker disciplined.

Sandra   And I'll tell you this. He seemed a helluva lot nicer than the pot-ugly trash you get policing the streets in America. And he said he would see me later.

Willie   I/

Rena *silences* **Willie** *by revealing a big jacket in the same material as the bagpipes and skirt.* **Rena** *holds the jacket up to* **Willie**. **Willie** *lets out a giant shocking sob.*

Rena   What's the matter with you? Do you not like it? (*To*

Sandra.) Because it's going to look smashing on him. Isn't it, Sandra?

Willie *lets out another sob.*

Rena   What is the matter with you?

Willie   I just want someone to love me!

They all look at **Willie** *in wonder and turn away in embarrassment. Brief bagpipe warm-up from off.* **Sandra** *picks up the manuscript.*

Sandra   Actually, you know, this looks quite good.

Rena   What is it, Sandra?

Sandra   Patrick's book.

Rena   What's it called?

Sandra   Family A – tro – cit – ies. Oh, *Family Atrocities* by Patrick Nauldie.

Bagpipes are now tuned up. We get 'Scotland the brave' on bagpipes from off. **Rena** *and* **Sandra** *look out as lights fade.*

Act Two

Willie *still seated as at end of Act One, dazed. Table now on, with wig, cap, framed photos and other presents laid out. A small cocktail cabinet facing* **Willie** *temptingly. He gradually comes to and sees cocktail cabinet. He gets up, searches the cabinet and finds well-used bottle of whisky. He opens it, takes a slug, recovers, takes another slug, recovers, goes to take a third slug when he discovers it is empty. He starts searching the cabinet.*

Rena *(off)* Aye, some help, Willie.

Willie Och, woman. Away and/

Rena *(off)* Some help, I said.

Willie Away and/

Rena *(off)* Some help with your furniture. (What?)

Willie Away and boil your tits.

He carries on searching as **Rena** *struggles in with an armchair.*

Where's my Scotch, woman?

Rena Oh, God knows.

Willie It was here.

Rena And never mind your Scotch.

Willie I had a full bottle.

Rena You've your work. (What?)

Willie So where is it?

Rena It's in your hand.

He looks at it.

Willie Och, woman.

He tosses bottle over his shoulder.

Where have you planked it?

Rena   I never touched your Scotch.

Willie   Aye, trust you, woman.

Rena   Just help me in with your furniture.

Willie   Trust you to clean my carpet.

Rena   Because it's that damned antiquated.

Willie   You'll've cleaned my carpet in a disorganised fashion and lost my Scotch. I/

Rena   It's that damned heavy.

Willie   You'll've lost it, Bridget, deliberately on purpose. Ha ha.

Rena   It's that damned/ What are you wanting your Scotch for? You've your work.

Willie   I'm not going back to work.

Rena   That's what you think, boy.

Willie   Bridget.

Rena   Because/ 'Bridget.'

Willie *goes off.*

Willie (*off*)   Ha ha.

Rena *goes out another way.* **Patrick** *comes in from one direction, with bag and bagpipes.* **Sandra** *from another.*

Patrick   Sandra!

Sandra   You bastard.

Patrick   Thank you.

Sandra   You hooligan!

Patrick   Thanks for the bagpipes.

Sandra   You criminal. (What?)

Patrick   Great sound on them!

Sandra   Don't mention it!

Sandra *puts down her cases.*

Patrick   You're going somewhere?

Sandra   I can't stand it here another minute!

Patrick   Aren't you?

Sandra   I know when I'm not wanted.

Patrick   Because where are you going?

Sandra   I'm getting the hell out of here!

Patrick *puts down bag and bagpipes,* **Sandra** *goes to go.*

Patrick   You're not giving up and going home to America?

Sandra   Where I go, Patrick Nauldie, is no affair of yours!

Patrick   I'm disappointed, Sandra.

Sandra   I/

Patrick   I had hopes for you.

Sandra   Och!

Sandra *goes to go.*

Patrick   So many wonderful hopes for you!

Sandra   I/ But how could you write those things about me?

Patrick   I thought we might discuss my book and/

Sandra   How could you write those things about them?

Patrick (What?)   And maybe even discuss changing your life.

Sandra   I'll discuss nothing with you.

Patrick   You didn't respond well to the truth?

Sandra   I was shocked.

Patrick   The truth can be shocking, of course. Ha.

Sandra   I was/ Ha!

Sandra *goes off in one direction.* **Rena** *comes in from another with another armchair.*

Rena   Have you cleaned out the bath, Patrick?

Patrick   Not yet, Mum.

Rena *positions the armchair.* **Patrick** *goes to go.*

Rena   Oh and Patrick?

Patrick   Yes, Mum?

Rena   Where's your father's cap?

Patrick   I/

He takes it out of his bag and gives it to her.

How did you get on with my book, Mother?

Rena   What book?

Patrick   My book, Mother! Has it changed your life?

Rena   Oh yes, Patrick. It has.

Patrick   In what way, Mother?

Rena   It's changed my arse.

Patrick   I/

Willie (*off*)   Bridget!

Patrick *goes off one way.* **Willie** *comes on another.*

Willie   Found my Scotch yet, Bridget?

Rena   Aye, never mind, Bridget. And never mind your Scotch.

Willie   Where is it?

Rena   When that cop comes back you've to be sober for him!

Willie   I've told you, Bridget!

Rena   You're not taking the afternoon off.

Willie   I'll take it off if I so choose.

Rena   You've never had an afternoon off in your life.

Willie   Because they're all at it these days.

Rena   You're the conscientious type!

She hands him his wig. He holds it in one hand. She hands him the cap.
He blocks that by handing her back the wig. She takes it. Then realises
what she has done. So she tries handing him the cap again. He takes it.
Then she realises she still has the wig. She hands him the wig. He takes
it. He puts the cap on. He puts the wig on top of the cap. She reaches to
fix them. He dives out of her way with unexpected agility. But the cap and
wig fall off in the process. He picks them up and gives them to her. She
returns them. He puts them on her head. She returns them. He throws
them away.

Willie   And where's that boy of mine, woman?

Rena   He's cleaning out the bath. For his mother!

Willie   I'll have to congratulate him!

Rena   You don't even like your son!

Willie   Congratulate him and apologise for not believing in
him!

Rena   You don't like your son taking your hot water for a
bath.

Willie   If my Patrick's the educated type he can take my hot
water till he's blue in the face. If he's educated he can drown
in my hot water. If he's educated he can shit all over my
carpet, Bridget.

Rena   I/

Willie   Because I love my son.

Rena   You can't start/

Willie   Where is he till I tell him?

Rena   You can't start loving Patrick.

Willie   Bridget.

Willie *picks up his wig, puts it on sideways and goes out.*

Rena   It's me that loves him! I/ 'Bridget!'

Willie (*off*)   Aye 'Bridget', Bridget!

Rena   I/ (*Shouts.*) Oh, Patrick! . . . Are you there?

Patrick *comes in with cleaning materials.*

Rena   And when you've finished cleaning the bath, son, could you show your old mother how much you love her and give her a hand to bring in his furniture.

Patrick   Yes, Mum.

Rena *goes off.*

Rena (*off*)   Thanks. Because you don't love him, son. Do you?

Patrick   No, Mum.

Patrick *goes to go.* **Sandra** *comes in with suitcases.*

Sandra   You wrote that my mother/

Patrick   Did you not like what you read?

Sandra   My own mother doesn't/

Patrick   Were you offended?

Sandra   She doesn't trust me.

Patrick   Well, she doesn't.

Sandra   Yes, but you didn't have to write it down for people to read!

Patrick   I/

Enter **Rena** *with a rug.*

Rena   Patrick Nauldie: have you finished cleaning out the bath yet?

Patrick   I'll do it now.

Patrick *exits.*

Rena   Are you going somewhere, Sandra?

Sandra   I was thinking of going back to America, Mother.

Rena   Well, help me in with his bureau before you go back to America.

Sandra   I/ No, I will not. And you won't either. You can just get your coat on and come back to America with me.

Rena   I'm not going to America, Sandra.

Sandra   Why not? Did Patrick put you off?

Rena   No. It wasn't Patrick that put me off. It was you. But if you decide to not to go back to America I'll maybe think of taking your place. Oh yes: Big Ronnie and me: perfect!

Sandra   He's not that good.

Rena   What's wrong with him?

Sandra   He's/ He/ He's got BO.

Rena   I'll wash him.

Sandra   He goes to church.

Rena   I'll go with him.

Sandra   He wears pyjamas in bed.

Rena   What do you expect, Sandra?

Sandra   What do you mean?

Rena   He's to go to bed with you every night.

Sandra *lets out a sob.*

Rena   I'm sorry, Sandra, I/

Sandra   Why is Patrick the favourite?

Rena   Oh, Sandra. You're my wee daughter.

Sandra   Why do you prefer Patrick to me?

Rena   And I do quite like you.

Sandra   Everything stops for Patrick.

Rena   It's not your fault if you're not popular.

Sandra   I/ Why did you send Patrick with special messages?

Rena   I did not.

Sandra   You did, Mother.

Rena   I/ How did you know?

Sandra   Patrick wrote about it in his book.

Rena   He what?

Sandra   He has, Mother. And a whole lot of other things.

Rena   Right!

Rena *goes to go.*

Sandra   Where are you going, Mother?

Rena   I trusted him with my special messages.

Sandra   I/

Rena   He's not supposed to be writing them in his book.

Sandra   Don't worry, Mother. He won't be publishing any of your special messages.

Rena   I hope not.

Rena *goes.*

Sandra   Because he'll be publishing that book over my dead body!

Patrick *comes in.*

Sandra   So it says in your book you kept one of these special messages.

Patrick   I did.

Sandra   You kept one you didn't deliver.

Patrick   That's right.

Sandra   And you never opened it.

Patrick   I didn't.

Sandra   Can I see it?

Patrick   What for?

She puts her hand out. **Patrick** *goes into his bag and brings out a letter which he shows to her. She tries to take it. He resists. She lets go. He gives her it. She studies it and holds it up to the light, laboriously. It's unmarked.*

Sandra   You seriously never opened it?

Patrick   No.

Sandra   And it says in your book you're going to give it back to her.

Patrick   When the time is right, yes.

Sandra   If you're going to do that do you not think we should open it?

Patrick   Why?

Sandra   In case it's important.

Patrick   Now you know why she doesn't trust you.

Sandra   What?

Patrick   I'm returning it to her, Sandra, unopened.

Sandra   It might be full of stuff she'd rather forget.

Patrick   We can't decide that.

Sandra   I/

Patrick   Now give it back.

Patrick *puts his hand out for the letter.*

Sandra   I/

Sandra *holds it up. He grabs it. She doesn't let go. He backs off. She hands it to him. He puts it in his bag.*

Patrick   How about some feedback then?

Sandra   What?

Patrick   What did you think about my book?

Sandra   Don't talk to me about your book.

Patrick   You didn't like it?

Sandra   Did I like it? Are you joking? It's one of the most offensive pieces of shit I've read in my entire life.

Patrick   OK. What about them?

Sandra   Oh, it's totally unsuitable for *them*.

Patrick   What?

Sandra   I'm not having them read your book, Patrick.

Patrick   You mean they've not read it?

Sandra   Of course they've not read it.

Patrick   I/

Sandra   It would kill them.

Patrick   Where's my book, Sandra?

Sandra   Never you mind where your book is.

Patrick   They've got to read it. They're the whole point.

Sandra   They'll never read your book, Patrick.

Patrick   I want to see the effect on them!

Sandra   You're not going to see their reaction to it, Patrick.

Patrick   I/ Why?

Sandra   I'm confiscating it.

Patrick   What?

Sandra   See you in court, wee brother.

Sandra *goes out.*

Patrick   I/ If you confiscate it, I'll confiscate you.

He goes to follow her. **Rena** *comes in with a lamp.*

Rena   Did you deliver all my special messages, Patrick Nauldie?

Patrick   Would I do anything to harm you, Mother?

Rena   Well, I hope you didn't write any out in that book of yours?

Patrick   Oh no. Your special messages were private, Mother.

Rena   That daughter of mine. Just because I'm not going to America with her, she's trying to upset me.

Patrick   I/

Rena   Right, Patrick. I'll take some help now.

Patrick   I/

Willie (*off*)   What's my Scotch doing there?

Rena   Patrick?

Patrick   Right away, Mother.

Rena *puts the lamp down and goes out.* **Patrick** *goes to follow her.*

Willie (*off*)   Was that you, Bridget? Because imagine concealing my Scotch in my gramophone. Aye, you're a/ I've a good mind to arrest you for that, Bridget.

Rena (*off*)   Never mind your Scotch. Just come and help me and Patrick.

Willie (*off*)   Bridget.

Patrick *opens one of* **Sandra**'s *cases and starts searching. Music comes on abruptly. 'Bimbo' by Jim Reeves.* **Patrick** *snaps the case shut in knee-jerk fear.* **Rena** *comes in with a coffee table.*

Rena   Who put that on?

Patrick   I/

Rena   Because get that off, Willie.

She puts the coffee table down.

You can't start putting your antiquated gramophone on in the kitchen. You'll get soap powder all over your antiquated records!

She goes out. **Willie** *sings along provocatively.* **Patrick** *goes into another case. The presents for the family in America fall out with a small paper bag.* **Patrick** *puts the presents away and closes the case. He goes to open another case when he finds the little bag. He picks it up and goes to repack it. At the last second he glances inside. He takes out a large box of condoms. The music stops abruptly. He conceals the condoms and listens.*

Willie (*off*)   Aw, Bridget!

Rena (*off*)   Aye, never mind 'Bridget'.

Patrick *relaxes and looks at the box of condoms.*

Willie (*off*)   Brid-get!

Patrick (*Reading*)   'Donger Kings.'

Rena (*off*)   You've got work.

Willie (*off*)   This is a celebration.

Patrick   'Extra-sensitive and ultra-safe.'

Rena (*off*)   Oh, celebrate your arse.

Patrick   'Your double-strength condom with/ '

Rena (*off*)   Just help me in with your gramophone!

Patrick   '– with contraceptive jelly.'

Patrick *puts the box in his pocket and goes to go. Music comes on again.* **Patrick** *changes his mind and looks in another case. Enter* **Sandra** *with more cases, unseen by* **Patrick**. *She is about to speak when she thinks better of it and retreats.*

Rena (*off*)   Will you get that noise off and help me?

Music stops again. **Patrick** *takes fright and snaps the case shut.*

Willie (*off*)   Aw, Bridget.

Rena (*off*)   Oh, don't bother. Here. Take this. Patrick! Some help, son!

Patrick *goes out.* **Sandra** *comes forward and puts down the cases.* **Sandra** *goes into one of the cases she has just brought in. She takes out* **Patrick**'s *manuscript, looking around, before hiding it in the cocktail cabinet. She looks at the cocktail cabinet for a second and puts it in a less conspicuous position maybe turned front on to the back of the room.*

Rena (*off*)   You ready, Patrick, son? Lift!

Patrick *and* **Rena** *come in with the gramophone.* **Willie** *comes in behind them with a lamp and a new bottle of Scotch, which he has evidently drunk from.*

Willie   And mind you don't mark my good gramophone.

Rena   I'll mark you if you don't shut your fat trap!

Willie   Bridget/

Rena   And see this house you're buying me, Patrick. Can it have all dark colour, high-quality carpets? Can it have/ ? Who put his cocktail cabinet there? Just put it down, son.

They put down the gramophone and pick up the cocktail cabinet.

Sandra   No, Mum. Don't move it.

Rena   What are you talking about, Sandra?

Sandra   It doesn't go there!

Rena   How long have I lived here, Sandra?

Sandra   It's better where it is.

Rena   I know where his effing furniture goes.

They put the cocktail cabinet down.

Sandra   And see you, Scots!

Willie   What about us Scots, America?

Sandra   You make me sick.

Rena *lets out a big sob.*

Sandra   I didn't mean you, Mother.

Willie   And watch the lip, America!

Sandra   You don't count.

Rena   I'm not bothered what you say, Sandra.

Sandra   What?

Rena   It's what I say.

Sandra   What did you say?

Rena   It's the first time I said a really bad word.

Sandra   I/

Willie   At one point lip like that would have made me aggressive. Ha ha.

Sandra   Oh, I'm sorry.

Willie   That's OK.

Sandra   I suppose.

Willie   Because, you see, Patrick, son: I'm a reformed character. Which is why I forgive you. Oh yes. I forgive you for all you've done to us. I forgive you and here's my cap!

He picks up his cap and gives it to **Patrick**.

Wear it till your heart's content, eh? No, go on. Are you not going to wear it, son?

Patrick   There's nothing wrong with me.

Willie   I/

Patrick   But there is with you. All of you. That's why you're all going to have to get away from each other.

Sandra   I/ What right have you got to tell us what to do?

Patrick I/

Willie Every right.

Sandra What right? Ah: excuse me!

Willie Because he's the educated type.

Sandra I'm a happily married/

Willie And because he's/

Sandra I'm a citizen of the United States of America!

Willie He's/

Sandra No one tells me what to do!

Willie He's written a book!

Patrick You haven't even read my book, Dad.

Willie That's why this is a/

Patrick And neither have you, Mum.

Willie This is a celebration!

Patrick Because Sandra stopped you!

Willie *takes a drink and goes to the gramophone.*

Rena I beg your pardon, Patrick Nauldie.

Sandra I stopped them reading it all right.

Rena Sandra didn't stop me reading it.

Sandra I read four and a half pages of this book.

Rena I just didn't fancy it.

Willie Your mother never was the educated type, Patrick. Ha ha. But then again, son, neither am I.

Willie *plugs in the gramophone.*

Patrick Four and a half pages?

Willie Ha ha.

Sandra   I read four and a half pages and it was four and a half pages *too bloody many*.

Willie   Ha ha.

Patrick   So no wonder you took my book personally.

Sandra   Yes, no wonder. Because you wrote that/

Patrick   What about the wider argument?

Sandra   You wrote that/

Patrick   The critique of family values?

Sandra   I/ Yes! You wrote that I'm a sadist!

Patrick   The/

Rena   So you are, Sandra.

Sandra   And he wrote that I was like a/

Willie   Aye, well done, Patrick.

Sandra   He wrote that the family had made me a/

Willie   This book sounds good. Ha ha.

Willie *takes a drink.*

Sandra   A/

Rena   At one point I thought I'd have to take you for treatment.

Sandra   A frustrated, caged animal!

Willie *starts searching for a record.*

Rena   Because do you remember the time I lent Patrick your bike one afternoon when he was only four and you were at school?

Sandra   I was not a/ Yes I do. Because that's in his book as well!

Rena   And then you got the afternoon off because of the teachers' strike?

Sandra   That was my bike.

Rena   And you chased after him with your skipping rope to get your bike back?

Sandra   So I chased after him all right.

Rena   And you whipped him.

Sandra   I/

Rena   Didn't she, Patrick?

Patrick   I/

Sandra   If I did whip him/

Rena   Didn't she, Patrick?

Patrick   I/

Sandra   If I did whip him/

Rena   That was sadistic, Sandra. (What?)

Sandra   If I did whip him, it just shows what a nice person I am to discipline my young brother and stop him riding down the wrong side of the road!

Patrick   Well, if you'd read my book, Sandra, you'd know that/

Sandra   It just shows that no matter what I do I'll never be as popular as Patrick.

Patrick   If you'd read my book properly, Sandra, you'd know that/

Sandra   And it just shows that the sooner I get the hell out of here the better.

Patrick   None of that's the point!

Sandra   I/

Willie   Exactly, son. Jim Reeves, everybody?

Rena   You're not playing records, Willie.

Willie   Records, Bridget. Ha ha.

Willie *goes to take a drink.* **Patrick** *snatches it elegantly from him.*

Patrick   Oh no you're not.

Willie   Eh? Oh aye.

Rena   Well done, Patrick.

Patrick   You're going to stay sober and read my book!

Willie   I should have offered but/

Patrick   So where is it?

Willie   Bridget'll have planked the glasses.

Patrick   Because if you don't read my book, how will you find out that isolation really works?

Pause.

Rena   We'll get this bureau in now.

Sandra   I'll help you.

Willie   You're going nowhere, both of you.

Sandra   I/

Willie   You're listening to Patrick.

Sandra   Why should I/ ?

Willie   Come on, Patrick: educate us.

Patrick   I/

Sandra   Why should I listen to him dragging up the past?

Willie   He'll be wanting to look back and learn, Sandra.

Sandra   The past should be forgotten.

Rena   Aye, maybe he'll be wanting us to look back and laugh, Sandra.

Willie   Tell them, Patrick.

Rena   Imagine me if I didn't laugh.

Sandra   I doubt if you'd like to read what he wrote about you.

Rena   I'd be pathetic like you, Sandra!

Willie   Aye, so you better find this book, America.

Rena   Aye, where's this book? Till I find out what he wrote about his old mother. Ha ha.

Sandra   Because I certainly can't forgive what he wrote about me.

Rena   'My mother was an old bag.' Probably. Ha ha.

Willie   The book, America.

Rena   Ha ha.

Sandra   So when this book comes out, I'm/

Willie   Just because you can't take a bit of educated criticism!

Sandra   I'm suing him and that's final.

Patrick   I/

Rena   Sandra Michigan.

Willie   Aye, and you sue my son/

Rena   You can't sue Patrick.

Willie   So if you sue my son/

Rena   Patrick's your wee brother.

Willie   So if you sue my son, America, I'll stand up in court and tell them every fat ugly word he wrote about you is true. Oh yes. I'll stand up in court and say I'm proud of my educated son. Because I'll stand up in court and flash my dick at the judge. Ha ha. Where's this book?

*He starts tossing open **Sandra**'s cases.*

Sandra   I/ Stop him.

She tries to stop him.

Rena   Don't bother stopping him, Sandra.

Sandra   I've got to get out of this/

Rena   He'll only get a search warrant.

Sandra   This hell.

Willie   She'll have my son's book planked.

He moves on to the case **Patrick** *took the condoms from.*

Sandra   I/ Oh no. Stop him, someone.

Patrick *restrains* **Willie** *by handing him the whisky back.* **Sandra** *tends to her case.*

Willie   Quite right, son.

Rena   I wish you'd all stop hindering me.

Willie *takes a drink.*

Willie   Cheers.

Rena   As if I didn't have enough to do.

Rena *adjusts furniture.*

Willie   Drink, anybody?

He offers the bottle round.

Patrick   Shut up.

Willie   Drink, Patrick?

Patrick   Shut your fat ugly drunken mouth.

Willie   I/

Rena   You tell him, son.

Patrick   You're a pathetic trapped woman-hater.

Patrick *takes the bottle back from him.*

Willie   There's no doubt about it.

Rena   I could have told you that, Patrick.

Willie   You're right about me. Of course, my experience of women was limited.

Rena   Willie Nauldie.

Willie   It took me thirty-odd years to learn about them.

Rena   Well, you know I/

Willie   Buy them a few trinkets.

Rena   I've always kept myself a secret from you.

Willie   Shut them up.

Rena   'Trinkets.'

Patrick   Exactly, Mother.

Rena   You know nothing about me. (What, son?)

Patrick   You had to.

Rena   Whereas I know everything there is to know about you. Ha ha.

Willie   Och, Bridget.

Rena   Things you don't know I know about you. Ha ha.

Willie   What's there to know? Ha ha.

Patrick   Exactly, Father.

Willie   What?

Patrick   Exactly.

Sandra   I'm just sick to death of being ignored.

Patrick   Exactly, Sandra.

Sandra   What?

Patrick   It's the family that's ignoring you. Because we're just not built to be together, are we? We want things we can't give each other. That's why Mum and Dad have separate rooms. So he can get away from her.

Willie (*singing*)   'I love you because you understand, dear.'

Rena   Oh, Patrick!

Willie   'Every little thing I try to do.'

Rena   He doesn't get away from me.

Willie   'You're always there to lend a helping hand, dear.'

Rena   I get away from him.

Willie   'But most of all I love you 'cause you're you.' Ha ha.

Patrick   You get away from each other. Because you must.
And it's a good thing. Separate rooms is the start of a natural
process leading to complete separation and freedom.

Sandra   What's natural about it? A wife should sleep with
her husband every night.

Patrick   Will someone please say something I can respect!

Willie   'No matter what the world may say about me.'

Patrick   I/

Willie   'I know your love will always'/ Aye see your respect,
Patrick. I'd love it.

Rena   Willie Nauldie.

Willie   Ha ha. I'd love it.

Rena   You've been a bad wicked pig all your life. You'll get
no respect from my son. Will he, Patrick?

Patrick   I/

Willie   Aye. And the next time I walk in the station I will no
longer go: 'No, Willie boy, cool it.' I'll go: 'See your arsehole,
Sergeant McIntyre, I'm going to stuff your thankless fucking
job right up it.' Ha ha. (*Sings.*) 'You're always there to lend a
helping hand, dear.'

Horn is tooted.

Willie   Aye, ya:/

Rena   Oh, Patrick.

Horn is tooted again.

Willie   Ya beauty, Sergeant McIntyre. Because/

Rena   Oh, Sandra.

Willie   Because that time is now.

Goes to go, taking the whisky from **Patrick**, *nonchalantly. Stops to adjust his wig but it still sits wrong.*

(*Sings.*) 'But most of all I love you 'cause you're you.'

He goes off.

Rena   I can't be expected to take any more of this.

Patrick   Where's my book?

Sandra   I'm not telling you where your book is.

Rena   He can't hand in his notice in that state, I said.

Patrick   Where is it?

Sandra   I'll give you it when I'm good and ready.

Rena   He can't hand in his notice like that.

Patrick   I'll look for it myself. (What, Mother?)

Rena   He'll get sacked for being drunk and disorderly.

Patrick   I/

Patrick *goes off.*

Car horn plays out a few notes from a crazy tune.

Rena   I can't be expected to take any more of this.

Sandra   What about me, Mother?

Rena   What about you?

Sandra   I want away.

Rena   Aye, away back to America.

Sandra   I don't want to go to America.

Rena   Give us all peace.

Sandra   I want to go where they drink Coke straight from the can, where your hair always stays in place in a high wind and where you can run the marathon with your period!

Rena   Oh, Sandra.

Sandra   What, Mother?

Rena   I won't be joining you.

More notes from the car.

Patrick (*off*)   What's going on out there?

Rena (*shouts*)   Oh, don't worry, Patrick son. Your father will just be dancing in the street. That's all. Him and his colleague will be sitting in the police car knocking back your father's Scotch.

Sandra   His colleague?

Rena   Yes. His colleague.

Sandra   Right, Mother.

Rena   What is it?

Sandra *goes.*

Sandra (*off*)   Don't wait up!

Patrick *comes in.*

Rena   What are you talking about, Sandra?

Patrick   Did you see what Sandra did with my book, Mother?

Rena   No, I didn't.

Patrick   You've not read any of it?

Rena   Where would I get time to read a book, Patrick?

Patrick   I/

Rena   What a relief when you get me out of here.

Horn goes again.

See what I mean? If it's not one thing it's another.

Patrick *goes out.*

Rena   So come and help me, Patrick.

She sees he is gone.

Patrick?

She goes to go as **Willie** *comes in, without his wig.*

You swine.

Willie   'Bobby,' I says to my colleague, 'come away in.'

Rena   You swine.

Willie   'Sample my hospitality. The wife'll make us up a sandwich.'

Rena   Aye, no more sandwiches.

Willie   'A sandwich, I says!'

Rena   And no more colleagues!

Willie   It's your rotten sandwiches'll've put him off, Bridget.

Rena   Aye and the drink wears off, Willie Nauldie, you go to your colleagues: 'Get to eff, you dirty bee, you.'

Willie *lurches towards her.*

Willie   Care for a dance, Bridget?

Rena   Only the actual words right out.

She dodges past him. He swerves and heads towards the gramphone.

Willie   Balderdash!

At the gramophone, he swerves and lands seated with startling uprightness in an armchair.

Rena   And who is it that has to run after your friends and apologise? ('Balderdash?')

Willie   But care for a dance, balderdash?

Willie *gets up and swerves towards* **Rena**. *She dodges. He swerves to gramophone and tries to put on a record.*

Rena   I'll balderdash you. There'll be no more balderdash. I'll be getting away from here soon. Whenever Patrick gets me fixed up with a house. Oh yes, Willie Nauldie, who'll be your slave then?

She goes to go. **Patrick** *comes in. This stops* **Rena** *in her tracks.*

Right, Patrick. Help me in with his/

Willie *scratches record noisily.*

Willie   Whoops. Ha ha. The human element.

Dances round the room, studying it for a scratch.

Care for a dance, Jim? Care for a/ ?

Patrick   How can you put up with this, Mother?

Rena   Och, Patrick.

Patrick   How can you?

Rena   Just help me in with his bureau!

Patrick   I/

Rena   Patrick!

Rena *goes out followed by* **Patrick**, *unseen by* **Willie**.

Willie   Care for a dance, Jim? No you don't do you? Fuck you then. Because fuck you.

He snaps the record in two. Horn goes again outside.

And fuck my family. They can't get away from me quick enough. And their father's bloody colleague drives off with their father's bloody married Yankee daughter and their father's bloody Scotch after refusing their father's bloody Scottish hospitality. And I don't hate women. Women hate me. Particularly if they're called Bridget. They walk out my bedroom and leave me. How dare you call me bald? I'm not bald. Yes I am bald. Bald and proud. And you weren't ever normal, Patrick. You didn't even like fishing.

Drops the snapped record and swerves to the gramophone.

Jim Reeves? I love you.

Takes out another record.

Give me a kiss, son. Aye, give me a big kiss.

He kisses the record avidly and puts it on the turntable.

And as for you, Bridget Balderdash, you kicked me out your bed for being a a baldy bastard. And you've got my house like a tip. So where's my furniture, Bridget? And, while we're not on the subject, you've set my son against me. All he cared about was his Bridget. His Bridget and his bagpipes. Bagpipes and more pocket money. More pocket money to pay for more bagpipes. Bagpipes coming out his Bridgets. Oh yes. And he didn't like fishing. And quite right too. See fishing: it's boring as bagpipes. Boring as balderdash. Boring as Bridget. Bridget and that house of hers. It'll be a bagpipes house. Ha ha. And he didn't like knitting.

Patrick *and* **Rena** *come in carrying the bureau, which they put down.* **Willie** *puts his arm across the turntable. The needle sticks.*

Willie   Bridget!

Rena   Get out the road, Willie.

Willie   Bridget.

Rena   You're in the road. And that gramophone's in the wrong place. That's where the bureau should be.

They put the bureau down. **Patrick** *goes over and gently nudges* **Willie** *to one side.* **Willie** *falls good-naturedly but with unexpected pzazz and lands on his back, back where he started beside the gramophone.*

Rena   Come on, Willie. You're in the way.

He sits up and is about to get up when he loses control and falls back down, now out cold.

Will you get up, Willie? You're keeping me back.

Willie *doesn't respond.* **Patrick** *gently taps him with his foot.*

Rena　Actually, Patrick. On second thoughts, just leave him.

Patrick　But he's in the way, Mother.

Rena　It's better just to leave him.

Patrick　No, Mother.

Rena　It gets me a rest. (What?)

Patrick　Never mind getting a rest. It's about time you stood up to him.

Rena　I can handle him. He's my Willie.

Patrick　Stand up to him. For once in your life. Go on. Make a breakthrough.

Rena　Don't you dare talk to your mother like that.

Patrick　I/

Rena　And stop keeping me back please. I've got things to do. I/

Rena *goes off one way as* **Sandra** *comes on from another.*

Sandra　Did you get that secret out of her?

Patrick　I did.

Sandra　What is it?

Patrick　I can't tell you.

Sandra　Why not?

Patrick　It's too embarrassing.

Sandra　Is it that bad?

Patrick　I couldn't even begin to tell you.

Sandra　You mean you're not going to?

Patrick　You definitely won't say anything?

Sandra   I'm not that bad, am I?

Patrick   Well. The thing is. Willie can't get an erection.

Sandra   Aw, I don't believe it. You are joking. Who told you?

Patrick   She did.

Sandra   She actually told you?

Patrick   She'll say anything to me!

Sandra   Oh no. Ha ha.

Patrick   And he's very embarrassed about it.

Sandra   Wow. Ha ha. I wish I was back in Fraserburgh, New Jersey now. They'd love that. Ha ha.

Patrick   Ha ha. Where's my book?

Sandra (*of* **Willie**)   What happened to him?

Patrick   The book, Sandra.

Sandra   Do you think he's all right? (What?)

Patrick   The book!

Sandra   Yes, I've been thinking about your book.

Patrick   Less bullshit. Hand it over.

Sandra   I/

Patrick   Because if you don't, I'll/

He produces condoms.

I'll show these to Mum and Dad.

Sandra   I/

Patrick   And don't pretend that doesn't cause you a problem. You were frantic when he attacked your case.

Sandra   I don't want him pawing my/

Patrick   I saw you.

Sandra   I'm ashamed of nothing.

Patrick   Who said anything about shame?

Sandra   You went into my case.

Patrick   The book!

Sandra   You took my fun present from Scotland for
Ronnie.

Patrick   The book! And I'll give you back your . . . fun
present from Scotland. For Ronnie.

Sandra *bursts into tears.*

Patrick   I/ Oh no! Stop this!

Sandra   Why is it me that gets the blame?

Patrick   I'm an independent human being.

Sandra   Why is it always me?

Patrick   You can't manipulate me with your emotions.

Sandra   Always, always me!

Patrick   All I wanted was for you to read my book.

Sandra   I'd be quite happy to read your book.

Patrick   Read my book and maybe even change your lives.

Sandra   I want to change my life!

Patrick   I/ What?

Sandra   I mean: the bit about husbands and wives almost
inevitably blocking out what is best in each other is/

Patrick   What are trying to say, Sandra?

Sandra   It's absolutely wonderful!

Patrick   Is it?

Sandra   Yes it is, Patrick Nauldie. Because I've found it so
true to my experience. I've found it so true. I mean: when I
got on that plane to America after you'd run away from home

like a coward. Yes, when I got on that plane to America, there was no book, there was no one there to warn me that Ronnie might be sitting next to me. Oh no. There was no one there to warn me that he might be the nicest guy in the whole wide world. There was no one there to warn me that if I married him when I got off the plane he'd stop being so nice and deliberately block out what's best in me. That he would block out what's best in me, after I'd had his children for him. No. And no one warned me that after I'd had his children for him I'd be too old to become an air hostess and travel. Because there was no one there to warn me that after I'd had his children for him I might start to hate them. And after I'd had his children for him no one warned me that I might start pissing about buying stupid fun presents from Scotland for him. Because I had the crazy idea they'd perk up the lousy rotten sex life he gives me. So that's why I wanted to admit to you that although it's true I did find some bits of your book a bit uncomfortable, I was honestly/ I was honestly trying to come round to them. So now what am I going to do? Because my father's colleague has offered to come round in his dinner break and take me to the Holiday Inn at the airport. Then when his shift's finished he's going to come round and spend a few days with me at the Holiday Inn at the airport. While I look for somewhere to live and give him time to dump the conniving ugly bitch he's been stupid enough to live with for the last eight years. And I want him to dump her. Because I want to live with him permanently at the Holiday Inn at the airport. Because I fancy him legless. And because I've never had a Scotsman.

Patrick So when did you find out you hate Ronnie and your children?

Sandra Just now.

Patrick What?

Sandra Your book made me realise.

Patrick I/

Sandra Yes, your wonderful book, Patrick. Because your

book tells me Ronnie blocks out everything that's best in me. I never knew that before! And it tells me what to do about the boring stupid spoilt brats Ronnie had by me. And it tells me what to do every time I think about them sitting round the breakfast table stuffing their stupid fat American faces. Yes and your book tells me I should leave Ronnie's children behind me and never think about them sitting round the breakfast table again, doesn't it?

Patrick   That's not exactly what my book is meant to/

Sandra   So your book is telling me exactly what I want to hear, isn't it?

Patrick   I/ Yes. I suppose so. Yes. Now where is it?

Rena (*off*)   Patrick?

Sandra   It's in the cupboard in my room. In among my old school things. You'll need to dig deep.

Patrick *runs out.*

Rena (*off*)   You were supposed to help me, Patrick.

She comes on with a lamp.

Rena   Where's Patrick?

Sandra   Looking for that stupid boring book of his.

Rena   Are you going to stop your brother's book getting published?

Sandra   I've changed my mind.

Rena   What?

Sandra   It's a wonderful book. It's changed my life.

Rena   What's changed?

Sandra   For a start I'm moving back to Scotland.

Rena   What for?

Sandra   I can't live without you, Mother.

Rena   You'll have to stop talking shite, Sandra.

Sandra   It's true. Because it's shown me I have to get out the kitchen and get a life! Because, let's face it, Mother, Scotland's the best place in the world, isn't it? And Scots are lovely people. Particularly the policemen.

Rena   If Scotland's so wonderful, Sandra, why didn't you bring my grandchildren with you to Scotland to meet me?

Sandra   I/

Rena   Did you forget them?

Rena *goes to go.*

Sandra   Where are you going?

Rena   Well, if you're moving to Scotland I'll have to go to America.

Sandra   To see your grandchildren?

Rena   No, Sandra.

Sandra   What for then?

Rena   To get away from you.

Sandra   I/

Patrick *comes in.*

Rena   Did you find that book, Patrick Nauldie?

Patrick   No, I didn't.

Sandra   I'm sorry, Patrick. I just couldn't resist five more minutes of you eating your wee heart out.

Patrick   I/

Sandra *gets the book out of the cocktail cabinet. She waves it provocatively close to* **Patrick** *who has put his hands out for it and hands it to* **Rena**.

Sandra   Here, Mother. Read it. It's a masterpiece.

Patrick   You only read four and a half pages. You can't say it's a/

Sandra   I/

Rena *flicks through it, peering and putting on a lamp to help.*

Patrick   You can't say it's a masterpiece.

Sandra   It's a masterpiece. So who wants to read more than four and a half pages?

Patrick   I/

Sandra   Get it read, Mother!

Rena (*reading*)   'Chapter Four. Bridget the Slave.' Who/ ? Who's this Bridget the Slave? I don't like the sound of her! She sounds like a/ Oh ha ha. That'll be me! Now. 'Further evidence of the impossibility of people successfully living together comes from my mother. She was made pathetic and passive by her attempts to keep control of my father's bullying temperament and her own unpredictable moods. I would take her to the jobcentre to try and encourage her to get work and become independent. Her confidence was so shattered she didn't even have the courage to go up for cleaning work.' Patrick, the problem wasn't confidence. The problem was I'd spent the whole week cleaning up after you and your father. That was quite enough, thank you. 'But at least it disgusted me so much that I immediately resolved to leave and I never came back.' Yes, maybe you could say cheerio next time, Patrick. 'The resulting frustration she took out on her children. She set us against each other. As a deliberate slight to my sister she sent me to deliver special messages.' Patrick Nauldie. I did trust you more than your sister. But not that much more. I sent you to deliver the special messages because I knew the sight of a pathetic wee boy would/ would/ would/ Whereas Sandra: well, let's face it: she was such an insolent wee bitch she'd only put people's backs up.

Patrick   I/

Rena   Now: 'Chapter Six. Constable Nauldie. The . . . Small . . . Time . . . Tyrant. The Small'/ Ha ha. Ha ha. I like the sound of this bit. Willie? Look at this, Willie. Come on.

She starts beating **Willie** *with the manuscript. He sits up. She jabs him in the face with it.*

Willie   Bridget! Heh! All right. All right. Give it a break, will you?

She stops jabbing him.

Rena   You've been a bad wicked pig all your life, Willie Nauldie. Come on. Read it. It'll change your life. It'll kill you.

Willie *peers at manuscript and puts on another lamp to help him read it.*

Willie (*reading*)   'My father's ways of maintaining power included keeping me so short of pocket money that when I wanted to save up for my own set of bagpipes, I had to steal fifty pence from his jacket pocket every week. They never found out about it.' That's where you're wrong, boy!

Patrick   You'd have done something if you'd known about it.

Willie   We did do something. We didn't increase your pocket money! Ha ha.

Rena   Ha ha.

Willie *gets up, ending up in another position, and puts on another lamp to help him read.*

Willie (*reading*)   'There was no disguising my parents' barren sexless marriage. I used to listen at their bedroom door for sounds of sexual activity. But it was always the same thing. Within a minute of them going to bed I would hear the loud snores of my father.'

Sandra   But I thought/

Rena   But we knew you were listening at the door. Willie just pretended to snore until you went to bed. Then we/ Then we/ Well, we just had a good laugh. Didn't we, Willie?

Willie   We did woman, aye.

Patrick   Yes. But when Sandra moved out Mother moved into her room.

Sandra   And that was because my father couldn't get an erection!

Willie   What did you say?

Rena   Sandra! Don't you dare talk to your father like that.

Sandra   But you've not to feel bad about it!

Willie   I've had erections/

Rena   Your father had/

Sandra   You can go for counselling these days!

Willie   I've had more erections than/ Counselling?

Rena   Your father had plenty of erections, Sandra. Too effing many.

Sandra   I/ But/ Patrick? You said/:

Rena   You've gone too far this time, Sandra.

Sandra   What?

Rena   You humiliated your father.

Sandra   That was Patrick.

Rena   What?

Sandra   He told me about my father's problem.

Rena   Och, Sandra. That's just Patrick's sense of humour. Ha ha.

Sandra   So why did you move into my room, Mother?

Rena   I/

Rena   I moved out because I couldn't take any more erections. Where did you get them all, Willie?

Willie   I/

Rena   Then when I found out about your girlfriend I didn't move back in.

Willie   I did not have a girlfriend.

Rena   I followed you.

Willie   What do you mean you followed me?

Rena   I followed you twenty-seven times, Willie Nauldie. From your office to the big houses on the other side of the park.

Willie   My what?

Rena   So. I soon put a stop to that. I sent Patrick with a letter.

Willie   I hope you didn't, woman.

Rena   I sent her a letter all right.

Willie   I sincerely hope not.

Rena   She was a threat to my family. (What?)

Willie   She was my scalp specialist.

Pause.

Willie   So I hope you didn't send any letter to that poor woman. She was restoring my hair.

Sandra   She never got Mum's letter. Don't worry, Dad, Patrick didn't deliver it.

Rena   I trusted you with my special message, Patrick Nauldie.

By now, **Willie** *is in another position and puts on another lamp to read.*

Willie (*reading*)   'Patrick Nauldie. Jailbird and Criminal. I became a criminal by accident. Through no fault of my own I found I didn't have enough money to eat or pay the rent. I went on to discover the criminal life was more exciting and adventurous than what was on offer from mainstream society. When I was eventually caught, tried and imprisoned I was, at first, shocked by the pain of my loss of freedom and the struggle to adapt to prison protocol. However, after my period of adjustment was complete I found the enforced isolation and discipline led to a self-knowledge and peace of mind I had never previously known.'

Rena   Ha ha. Yes, my Patrick always was the writing type.

Willie (*reading*)   'And in conclusion I have begun to find my prison career so satisfying and preferable to the shapeless and chaotic random pairing of the world outside I will be sorry to see it discontinued.'

Rena   Even as a child he used to sit at his father's bureau and write a load of shite.

Sandra   It's all right, Mum. Patrick'll be reformed now. Aren't you, Patrick?

Patrick   No, Sandra. I'm sorry. Well, it was an emergency. To be with you all today I had to steal a wee car. I'll take it back. I'll/

Rena   Well, don't you worry, Patrick son. You've betrayed your old mother right, left and centre. But all the same, whether you're a rapist, a murderer or even just a wee car thief, I'll still stand by you.

Sandra   You're awful quiet, Patrick.

Patrick   What of it?

Sandra   You came home to settle scores, didn't you?

Patrick   Oh no. I came home to get you all to change.

Sandra   So why don't you get on with it?

Patrick   I don't get on with it, Sandra, because though I did reckon on you all being irrelevant to each other I didn't on you not caring a toss about it. You'd rather be irrelevant to each other and drag out your miserable rotten lives together than face the pain of change.

Sandra   That's more like it, Patrick. You tell them.

Willie   Patrick Nauldie. You're under arrest.

Willie *moves towards* **Patrick**. **Patrick** *dodges him*.

Patrick   You're not arresting me, Dad. I'm walking out of here alone.

Willie   You're not walking out. I'm throwing you out.

Willie *moves towards* **Patrick**. **Patrick** *dodges him.*

Patrick   You're not throwing me out. I'm leaving of my own accord.

Willie   You're not leaving of your own accord. You're leaving in a police van.

Willie *goes to phone and picks it up.* **Patrick** *knocks him clean away from the phone and* **Willie** *collapses.*

Patrick   I'm not leaving in a police van. I'll drive to the police station and give myself up.

Rena   Yes, maybe you should give yourself up, Patrick. Prison's the best place for you. You're a criminal.

Patrick *produces knife.*

Rena   See what I mean?

Patrick *seems to advance towards* **Sandra**. **Rena** *jumps in front of* **Sandra** *to protect her.*

Rena   You'll have to kill me first, Patrick Nauldie.

Patrick *swerves past her nonchalantly and cuts the telephone wire.*

Rena   Well, Patrick Nauldie. You might have blackened my name in that book of yours, even so I'll still take that house you promised me. When am I getting it?

Patrick   I didn't promise you a house.

Rena   What?

Patrick   I was trying to empower you to get your own house.

Rena   You've let your mother down, Patrick Nauldie. Even when the royalties from this book come through you wouldn't get your mother out of here?

Patrick   My book's not getting published.

Rena   What?

Patrick   It's not worth publishing.

Sandra   Well, I'm changing, Patrick. Thanks to your book.

Patrick   You, were changing long before my book, Sandra.

Sandra   What?

Patrick *takes out the condoms.*

Sandra   Oh no, Patrick. Please. Not here. I/

Patrick   Fun present from Scotland? For Ronnie? (*Reads.*)
At $8.50 a packet?

He throws the condoms down.

Rena *picks up the condoms.*

Rena   Could I perhaps have one of your wee American
johnnies, Sandra? I'll go out and get myself a man for the
night!

Sandra   I/

Patrick (*to* **Sandra**)   You definitely started changing before
you read my book.

Sandra (*to* **Patrick**)   I bought those things in America in
case your book changed me.

Patrick   You didn't know there was a book.

Sandra   Oh yes I did.

Patrick   What?

Sandra   Well I didn't. Well I did. I didn't know how I knew,
I just knew. I mean:/ I had no idea whatsoever why I went
into the pharmacy at the airport. Or why I bought these
disgusting/ these/ I do now though. But then, when I get
here, through no fault of mine, it turns out you've become a
prude and a weirdo and a loner. You're a person who doesn't
need people!

Patrick   It's needing people that makes people liars!

Sandra   It's lying that makes people happy.

Patrick   It's needing people that stops people changing.

Sandra   Well, I don't care what you say, Patrick, your book changed me. I'm out for what I can get in future. So I think you should reconsider getting it published.

Patrick   Who'd publish it?

Sandra   What it did for me, it could do for/

Patrick   Who'd publish it?

Sandra   America! America will publish it. People like changing their life in America.

Patrick   But it's complacent, inaccurate, rose-tinted rubbish.

Sandra   They like complacent, inaccurate, rose-tinted rubbish in America.

Patrick   That must be why I hate America!

Sandra   That's why *I* hate America. I hate everything American. American johnnies.

She picks up the condoms and tears them in two.

Patrick   That's enough, Sandra.

Sandra   American brats!

She takes down the photographs of her children and jumps on them.

Patrick   That's enough.

Sandra   And as for American bagpipes.

She picks up the bagpipes and starts tearing them apart.

So I'm never going back to America!

He tries to get them off her. But they burst open spectacularly. Stuffing, material and pipes flying all over the carpet. **Willie** *stirs during this and gets up.*

Rena   I/ You're making a mess of his carpet, Patrick.

Willie   That's my carpet, Patrick.

Willie *hits* **Patrick**.

Rena   His carpet.

Willie   My carpet.

Willie *hits* **Patrick**.

Rena   His carpet.

Willie   My carpet.

Willie *hits* **Patrick**, *a knockout blow, and* **Patrick** *collapses.* **Willie** *turns away and* **Sandra** *goes to tend* **Patrick**. **Rena** *watches this and starts to clean up the mess, putting the remains of the bagpipes on* **Patrick**'s *bag.*

Rena   So I might just come with you to America after all, Sandra. It's awful violent in Scotland.

Willie *picks up the phone, goes to dial and finds the cut wire.*

Willie   At one point if I'd've found my phone out of order I'd've hit someone. Ha ha.

He puts phone down.

Aye, you've been awful unlucky with your family, Bridget. I'll miss them all the same, when they finally fuck off. Ha ha. Where's my Scotch?

Having taken one of **Patrick**'s *boots off,* **Sandra** *opens the bureau to reveal the Scotch to* **Willie**. **Willie** *takes the Scotch with glasses to table.* **Sandra** *takes off the other boot and finds the special message.* **Sandra** *opens it and takes out a letter.*

Sandra (*reading*)   'Dear Miss.'

Rena   What's that, Sandra?

Sandra   Your special message, Mother.

Rena   Don't read it out. I was young and stupid when I wrote it.

Sandra   It'll show how much you've moved on, Mother. (*Reading.*) 'I thought you might like to know that I have frequently followed Willie from his place of work to your house. I have watched him enter your house and leave one hour later. I thought you might like to know my Willie puts his willie into many different women. They tend to be the type of women who have a large number of willies put into them. And I know for a fact he never washes his willie afterwards. That's why I personally never let my Willie put his willie into me. This is being delivered to you by my nine-year-old son. Just thank him. No reply necessary. PS I always try to see the funny side of things.'

Willie   I have never heard such a load of poppycock. Poppyseed. Copycat. Talking shop. Throbbing cock. Yes that's it. I've never heard such a load of throbbing cock in my life. Ha ha.

Willie *selects a record and puts it on the turntable ready.*

Sandra   I definitely think you should still try and get away from him, Mother.

Rena   I can't see me as a sad and lonely single person, Sandra.

Sandra   Why not, Mum? We're all sad and lonely these days! Being a sad and lonely single person is the height of fashion.

Willie *is pouring two whiskies.* **Rena** *picks up the condoms.* **Patrick** *starts to rouse and get up. She puts the condoms into* **Willie**'*s pocket.*

Rena   Do you still want me back, Willie?

Willie   Bridget.

Rena   You're a wonderful man. I don't deserve you.

Willie   Not bad yourself, Bridget. Shame about that family of yours! Get this frock thing on.

Willie *picks up and gives* **Rena** *her skirt.* **Rena** *hands* **Patrick** *his bag without eye contact. He takes it.* **Willie** *puts on the jacket.* **Rena** *puts on the skirt.* **Willie** *hands her a whisky and they drink. Horn is tooted.*

Sandra   Ready, Patrick?

Willie *turns on music.* **Sandra** *and* **Patrick** *pick up luggage. They turn to say goodbye.* **Willie** *and* **Rena** *put their drinks down.*

Sandra/Patrick   I/

Music begins. **Willie** *and* **Rena** *partner up and set forth on a nimble, skilful dance. It should be no less than entrancing.* **Sandra** *and* **Patrick** *slip out as the lights fade slowly.*

The Sex Comedies

The Sex Comedies premiered at the Traverse Theatre, Edinburgh, in February 1992.

The plays were performed in an ensemble with the following actors: Daniella Nardini, Paul Thomas Hickey, John Kazek, Alexis Kesselaar, Andy Manley and William Lesley.

The production was directed by Iain Reekie

The Lodger

Characters

Man, *early fifties*
Woman, *early fifties*

Setting

A room with a dust sheet on floor.

Woman *comes in with a tray of paint and a stool, wearing overalls, carrying small and large paint brushes. She puts stool down and stirs paint.*

Man *comes in with tray of paint and a stool, wearing overalls, carrying small and large paint brushes. He puts stool down, goes to stir paint but thinks better of it.*

Man　You didn't say you'd get the paint.

Woman　I'm the best at painting.

Man　I said I'd get the paint.

Man *starts stirring.*

Woman　How come you're home early?

Man　They start phoning at six o'clock.

Woman　I said I'd come home early.

Man　At six o'clock it'll get hectic.

Woman *stops stirring, goes to start painting the wall and thinks better of it.*

Woman　They *won't* start phoning at six o'clock.

Man　They will. (I put six o'clock in the advert.)

Woman　*You* didn't put the advert in.

Man *stops stirring and starts painting.*

Woman　I put the advert in.

Man *stops painting.*

Man　Well, you might have told me you were putting the advert in.

Woman　I said: 'I'm putting the advert in for five thirty.'

Man　That would have saved *me*/ Five thirty?

Woman　Five thirty.

Man　We said I was putting the advert in. (For six o'clock.)

Woman *starts painting.*

Man   Five thirty means we'll hardly have time to get started.

Woman   We have started.

Man   Before all the phone calls come.

Woman   At least *I've* started.

Man   You're missing bits out.

Woman   My painting's immaculate.

Man   You'll have to give your bits a second coat.

Woman   Missing bits out is the height of fashion.

Man   A second coat takes longer than/ The height of fashion?

Woman   It's the country-cottage look.

Man *and* **Woman** *start painting,* **Man** *markedly slower but more thorough than* **Woman**. *After we establish that,* **Woman** *stops.*

Woman   You're going too slow.

Man   I'm a perfectionist.

Woman   At that rate we won't get it finished tonight.

Man   I like to do a thing well.

Woman   At that rate we couldn't even ask the callers to call tomorrow.

Man   At least when the callers do call they'll be able to see a job well done.

Woman *starts painting. After a few seconds,* **Man** *stops.*

Man   What's the hurry about getting the callers to call tomorrow?

Woman   We want to let the room as soon as possible.

Man   I want to take my time and find the right tenant.

Woman   The sooner we let the room the sooner we'll be

able to *afford* a country cottage.

Man *starts painting.*

Man   So I hope you put 'Friendly and lively' in the advert.

Woman   I hope *you* put 'Friendly and lively' in the advert.

Man   I hope you put 'A young woman who is willing to muck in'.

Woman   Well, I hope *you/* A young *woman?*

Woman *stops painting.*

Man   Yes.

Woman   I put 'A young *man* who's willing to muck in'.

Man *stops painting.*

Man   But young men never pay the rent!

Woman   Oh? Young *women* take over the *bathroom.*

Man   Young men don't *flush the toilet.*

Women   Young women leave their *underwear* lying about.

Man   Young men go about the house *naked.*

Pause.

Woman/Man   So we might as well call the whole thing off.

Pause.

They put down their paint things.

Man   If we call the whole thing off what about our peace and quiet?

Man *picks up paint things and paints a cottage on the wall.*

Woman   Yes, what about our idyllic setting?

Woman *paints on trees.*

Man   Our view of the hills?

Man *paints on hills.*

Woman   Our water from a stream?

Woman *paints on a stream.*

Man   What about our time for decent conversation?

Man *splashes paint on* **Woman***'s breasts.*

Woman   Our time to be together at last?

Woman *splashes paint on* **Man***'s genitals.*

They go back to reload their brushes.

Man   But you don't really want a young man?

Woman   And you can't be serious about a young woman?

Man   Do you?

Woman   Can you?

Man   Young men.

He paints on a face covered with spots.

They've got skin like the surfaces of the moon.

Woman   Young women.

She paints on a face. And leaves it blank.

They've got no personality.

Man   I/

Woman   *And* no shape.

She paints on a vertical line beneath the face.

Man   Young men have got no finesse.

He paints on an identical line, then angles it up abruptly.

Woman   Young women fake their orgasms.

She paints on a voice bubble with 'ooh, ooh' in it.

Man   Young men ejaculate too soon.

He splashes on paint from tip of his angled line.

Woman   So I don't see what you see in young women.

Man   I don't see what you see in young men.

Woman   Young men remind me of you when you were younger.

Man   Young women remind me of *you*.

Woman   Oh? In what way?

Man   You had tits like a pair of Ming vases.

Man *crosses and paints them on* **Woman**'s *figure.*

Woman   You had a chest like a shagpile carpet.

She paints on a triangle to represent his torso with a mass of hair at the top.

Man   You had an arse like a cream meringue.

He paints on an arse.

Woman   Thanks very much. You had balls that dangled halfway to your knees.

She paints on balls.

Man   Don't mention it. You'd a cunt like a centrally heated boudoir.

He paints it on. (Correcting hers.)

Woman   You'd a cock like a tusk in a mink glove.

She paints it on. (Correcting his.)

I was so lucky.

Man   So was I.

Woman   Those were the days.

They put down their paint things. They spin together.

Man   Young people today don't match up.

Woman   Young people today are boring.

Man   Conservative.

Woman   Reactionary.

Man   Dowdy.

Woman   Inhibited.

They kiss.

So let's readvertise.

She takes phone off hook.

Man   Someone of our own age.

Woman   Someone of like mind.

Man   Of like *body*.

They sit, obscuring picture.

Man (*to audience*)   Someone who enjoys threesomes.

Woman (*to audience*)   Someone who appreciates murals.

They lie down, revealing complete picture.

The Cake

Characters

Archie
Danny

With a couple of simple switches, *The Cake* may also be played by two women.

Setting

A room with a table and chairs. On the table is a round uncut cake and a knife.

Danny *picks up the knife and goes to cut the cake.*

Archie   Don't.

Danny   Eh?

Archie   Don't cut the cake.

Danny   Why not?

Archie   Not yet!

Danny   I was going to cut it three ways.

Archie   Not till she comes

Danny   I was going to make three equal portions.

Archie   You might embarrass her.

Danny   Three equal portions will *save* embarrassing her.

Archie   She might not want to eat a third of the cake and leave it and/

Danny   She might be embarrassed about saying how much she'll want to eat and/

Archie   And get embarrassed.

Danny   And go hungry.

Pause. He puts down the knife.

I *know* your game.

Archie   I'm only being considerate.

Danny   I know your game, by the way.

Archie   I'm only being considerate, by the way.

Danny   You only want to eat more than your fair share of the cake.

Archie   I was being *very* considerate when I invited her round for the cake. —

Danny   It was me that saw her, in the baker's.

Archie　Aye, but it was *me* that talked to her.

Danny　It was me that found out she was lonely.

Archie　It was me that *asked her round* to share the cake.

Pause.

How do you know she's lonely?

Danny　She lives alone.

Archie　She might not/

Danny　She *said* she lives alone.

Archie　She might not *be lonely*.

Danny　And *I'm* not lonely because/

Archie　Well, sometimes I'm lonely and/

Danny　Because I *don't* live alone.

Archie　And I *don't* live alone.

Pause.

Do you think she'll come?

Danny　What?

Archie　I'm not sure if she'll come.

Danny　*She said* she'll come.

Archie　That doesn't mean she'll come.

Danny　A person says they'll come they'll come.

Archie　Not necessarily.

Pause.

Danny　Why *shouldn't* she come?

Archie　She might have been being polite.

Danny　No.

Archie　She might have been too embarrassed to say 'no'.

Danny   No.

Archie   She might have thought we were lonely.

Danny   No. (We're *not* lonely.)

Archie   She might have thought we were *desperate*.

Pause.

Danny   We're not lonely. We live together.

Archie   Well, Danny.

Danny   What, Archie?

Archie   Sometimes I'm lonely.

Pause.

Anyway:/

Danny   So she says she'll come, she'll come.

Archie   She said she'd phone if she wasn't coming.

Danny   Oh, well then:/ . . .

Archie   Oh, well then what?

Danny   Oh, well then *she'll phone if she's not coming.*

Archie   Not necessarily.

Danny   Yes.

Archie   No.

Danny   A person says they'll phone to say they're not coming, a person/

Archie   She might have been being polite.

Danny   A person phones to say they're not coming.

Archie   She might be too embarrassed to come.

Danny   No.

Archie   Yes. Too embarrassed to come *at all*.

Pause.

Danny   Why should she be too embarrassed to come *at all*?

Archie   She might not have fancied *you*.

Danny   Pardon?

Archie   She might have thought she had to sleep with you.

Danny   What?

Archie   Even though it was me she fancied. (Obviously.)

Danny   Eh?

Archie   She might have thought I was procuring her for you.

Danny   Haw, wait a minute.

Archie   Because procurement is probably the only way an ugly charmless bastard like you could get anything.

Danny   Oh, but Archie.

Archie   And she probably worried because she'd be too embarrassed to say no to the procurement after we'd invited her round and given her a cake. (What?)

Danny   Why does she have to sleep here *at all*?

Archie   Because I want her to sleep here.

Danny   Why?

Archie   Because I want her to sleep here *with me*.

Pause.

Danny   That's not fair.

Archie   I want her to sleep here with me because: *sometimes I'm lonely*.

Danny   Because if she has to sleep here I'd like us all to sleep together.

Pause.

Phone rings.

They don't answer it.

What did you say it meant again if the phone rings?

Archie   It means she's ringing up to say she's not coming.

Danny *picks up the knife to cut the cake.*

Archie   Don't

Danny   Why not?

Archie   Don't!

Danny   I was going to cut the cake in two.

Archie   Don't.

Danny   Why not?

Archie   Because I *don't want* any.

Pause.

Danny *puts the knife down.*

Danny   Yes, but what do you mean, you're lonely?

Phone continues to ring as lights fade.

Total Strangers

Characters

Woman
Man
Waiter

Setting

Café table, two chairs.

Woman *comes in, looks round, she sits at table, settles, looks at watch, settles.* **Waiter** *comes in, goes to table, smiles.*

Woman   I will be joined.

Waiter *smiles and goes to go.*

Woman   Perhaps I could just . . .

Waiter *turns.*

Woman   While I'm waiting for . . .

Waiter *returns and smiles.*

Woman   White wine, I think. Yes, white wine. A glass.

Waiter *smiles and goes.* **Woman** *watches him go, settles, looks round, goes into handbag, takes out face mirror, looks, gets absorbed in arranging front of hair. Once that activity is established,* **Man** *comes in, stops, looks round, spots* **Woman**, *makes a silent beeline, sits. He watches her. She senses his presence. As she lowers mirror, he turns away. She takes him in, seems about to speak, changes mind, puts mirror in bag and puts bag down. Looks away. Pause.* **Man** *looks at her. Pause. He grins. Senses her sensing his look and looks away. We see her gather herself. She turns to him.*

Woman   Excuse me. I am expecting to be joined.

Man   That's right.

Woman (*pause*)   Ah. I think we *will* want to sit. *Here.* At *this* table. (Sorry.)

Man   That's all right. This table's all right.

Woman (*pause*)   I don't think you understand. I'm *expecting* someone. Any . . . minute . . . now.

Man   You're expecting someone?

Woman   Yes. So if you don't mind, I/

Man   You're expecting someone *else*?

Woman   I/ Of course. I mean – I beg your pardon – what do you mean by 'someone else'? I/ That is: someone else as well as *who*?

Man   'Someone else as well as who!' Are you joking? Someone else as well as *who do you think*? Someone else as well as *me*.

Woman   But ah – excuse me – I'm not expecting *you*.

Man   That's where you are wrong.

Pause.

Woman   Don't worry.

Man   I won't.

Woman   *I'll* find another table. (*Shouts.*) Waiter.

Man   No problem.

Woman   I'll move.

Man   I'll come with you.

Woman   You can't. I mean: why would *you* want to come with *me*? We're strangers.

Man   *I know* we're strangers. *Of course* we're strangers. That's the *whole point*. This is *our first meeting*. A meeting of strangers. Interested in getting to know each other et cetera. But if you've changed your mind about meeting a stranger I'm sure he'll get you another table.

Waiter *comes in with wine glass.*

Man   Won't you?

Waiter *gives it to her.*

Waiter   Would you like another table?

Woman   No, I certainly would not. I certainly/

Waiter *turns to man and smiles.*

Waiter   Are you ready to order?

Man   Make it a beer.

Waiter *smiles and goes.*

Woman   I would never have believed it.

Man   It's true.

Woman   You can't be.

Man   I am.

Woman (*warming*)   You look *nothing like* your photograph.

Man   Why? What photograph have you got?

Woman   Don't you know?

Man   Why should I?

Woman   I would have thought you would have taken care over which photograph you/

Man   Why? Are you disappointed with me? (In the flesh?)

Woman   Oh ho ho. Oh ho ho no. It's not a question of disappointment. It's just – you look – if you don't mind my saying so – *absolutely nothing* like your photograph.

Man   No?

Woman   No!

Man   Can you make the adjustment?

Woman   I/

Pause.

Let me just . . . (*Goes into bag.*) Just as a matter of . . . (*Finds photo. Looks back and forward at it and him.*) It looks *even less* like you than I remember. (*He puts hand out. She passes it over. A suggestion of hand contact. He studies it with 'care'.*)

Man   You're right. It's nothing like me. A likeness less like me I find hard to imagine. That's because it's not me.

Woman   I/

Waiter *comes in with beer. Smiles. They smile back. He puts it down. Goes.*

Woman   It's not you?

Man   No.

Woman (*pause*)   You're sure?

Man   Oh no.

Woman   Oh. (*Pause.*) So who is it?

Man   Bill, I expect. Bill, by the looks of it. I would say it's almost certainly Bill.

Woman (*pause*)   This is Bill?

Man   Yes. (I'll plump for yes.)

Woman   Let me get this clear. *You* are *not* Bill?

Man   Me Bill?

Woman   Yes.

Man   *Me Bill?*

Woman   *Yes.*

Man   Where did you get the idea I could be Bill? Because no way could I be Bill. Bill's blond, well mannered and intelligent. (By all accounts.)

Woman   I know he is. *I* asked for him. (Or someone like him.) I/

Man   Whereas *I'm* dark, rude, ugly and stupid.

Woman   You/ No, you're not, you/ I mean:/

Man   I am. I am. You'd've preferred Bill.

Woman   No, not at all. I/

Man   You'd've definitely preferred/

Woman   I don't know how you can say that. I haven't even met Bill. I haven't/

Man   So you prefer me?

Woman   I/ You/ Ah ha ha ha.

Man   Ah ha ha ha.

Woman   Ah ha ha ha. Seriously though: what I want to know is: how could they just send . . . another . . . another . . . a substitute without first warning me that/

Man   So you *would* rather be with Bill.

Woman   I/ You/ You keep/ *I didn't say that.* I/

Man   You're disappointed.

Woman   I'm not. I/

Man   *I knew* you'd be disappointed.

Woman   You/

Man   I'll go.

Woman   No! I mean: you can't do that. I paid my money. I have a right to meet . . . *somebody*. I/ I mean: I have *a right to know* why they didn't first warn/

Man   Bill met someone.

Woman   Why they/ ? I beg your pardon.

Man   Bill met *someone else*.

Woman   I don't understand.

Man   He met someone else. He liked her. He didn't want to come. He couldn't face telling them. They didn't know he wasn't coming. They couldn't tell you. That's what Bill's like. You'd've hated him. You had a narrow escape. You should thank your lucky stars. You should thank God. You should/

Woman   Who are you?

Man   A friend of Mark's.

Woman (*pause*)   Mark?

Man   Yes. He's a friend of Raphael's.

Woman   I/ (*Pause.*) Raphael?

Man   A friend of Jim's.

Woman   And is Jim a friend of Bill?

Man   No.

Woman   I don't believe this. I just can't/ Who – then – *is* a friend of Bill?

Man   Nobody.

Woman   *Nobody?*

Man   You've seen how unreliable Bill is. Who *would* be his friend? No, Jim has the misfortune to be Bill's *cousin*. Are you with me?

Woman   No, I'm *not* with you. I've had no explanation about how *you* came to be here. (In Bill's place.)

Man   Do you need one?

Woman   Of course I need one.

Man   Why?

Woman   I don't believe you asked that. How *could* you ask that? Obviously I want to know how I came to be sitting here with a total stranger.

Man   Bill would have been a total stranger.

Woman   A *prepared* total stranger.

Man   Were you prepared for Bill's non-appearance?

Woman   I/

Man   His *unilateral* non-appearance?

Woman   You/

Man   So *does* it matter?

Woman   I want to know how my whereabouts tonight fell into your hands.

Man   It's a long boring story.

Woman   *I want to know.*

Man (*pause*)   Apparently, Bill told Jim he wasn't turning up. He'd met someone else he liked. So Jim asked to see your photograph.

Woman   Bill showed this . . . Jim . . . *my* photograph?

Man   Yes.

Woman   He broke the protocol of confidentiality?

Man   Shredded it. Smeared it. *Shat* on the protocol of confidentiality. (What a guy, uh? What a/) So you *minded* Jim taking a look at your photograph?

Woman   I don't want a/ Someone or other looking at me/ I gave no consent for/ I certainly have no desire to be *paraded*. People will think I do this sort of thing normally. I assure you I don't.

Man   Neither do I.

Woman   I've never done it before.

Man   Neither have I.

Woman   And I'll certainly never do it again.

Man   I won't either. (Certainly.) You're the first stranger I've ever met. But I'm quite enjoying it. (All the same.) Aren't you?

Woman   I/ That's not the/ The point *is*: *where* is my photograph *now*?

Man   I've got it.

Woman   *You've got it?*

Man   Yes. *I've* got it. Do you mind.

Woman   Yes I do. I mean: no I don't. I mean: give me my photograph and I'll go.

Man   Absolutely. (*Takes out photograph.*) You'll *go*?

Woman   I'll go if I want to go.

Man   Do you want to go?

Woman   How can you *say* that? How can you *assume* it's as *easy* as that? I'm not leaving until you tell me *how* you got my photograph!

Man   Mark gave it to me.

Woman   Mark?

Man   My friend.

Woman   I know he's your friend. How did Mark get my photograph?

Man   After Bill gave it to Jim, Jim decided he wasn't interested.

Woman   No?

Man   You're not his type.

Woman   I see.

Man   Does that bother you?

Woman   I/ You/ How would I know if it bothers me? I don't know him. I mean: of course it doesn't bother me. What an idea. 'I'm not his type.' *He's* certainly not *mine*.

Man   You don't know him.

Woman   Nor do I want to. Continue.

Man   Do you want me to?

Woman   I know *you* want to. Don't let *me* stop you.

Man   I won't. So anyway: Jim gave it to Raphael. (Raphael's got more varied taste than Jim.) And Raphael wouldn't have minded you. (As it turned out.)

Woman   Oh he wouldn't?

Man   No. But he couldn't make the time. He was working.

Woman   What a pity.

Man   Do you think so?

Woman   What did Raphael do with my photograph?

Man   He gave it to Mark.

Woman   And was Mark working too, I suppose?

Man   No. Not at all. But he thought you were the ugliest, stupidest-looking bat he'd ever seen in his life. Ha ha.

Woman   Ha ha.

Man   Ha ha.

Woman   How did you get my photograph?

Man   Mark gave it to me as a joke.

Woman   Oh he did?

Man   He did. But what old Mark forgets is: I'm a much nicer person than him. *I like personality.* And I could tell by your photograph you had some. Yes, I definitely felt from your photograph you could be worth a saunter. (*Pause.*) I told you it was long and boring.

Woman   It wasn't long *or* boring.

Man   No?

Woman   It was one of the most disgraceful episodes in the modern era. I refuse to be a commodity. So if you'll give me my photograph I'll/

Man   You're not staying?

Woman   Of course not. You're not who I expected.

Man   Do you think *you're* who *I* expected?

Woman   Who did *you* expect?

Man   How should I know *who* I expected? It's history. All I *do* know is: I've spent all this time and energy to be with you tonight and now you're going. You're actually getting up and going and leaving me! Aren't you?

Woman   I am. Yes. Sorry. The photograph!

Man   Do you have any idea what it took to expose myself like this to you? (A *total stranger*!)

Woman   You? *You?* Oh yes. It has to be about *you*. It's always about what *other* people are suffering. It's never about what *I'm* suffering. What about *me*. Submitting *my* photograph. *In all good faith*. Only to have it *shunted about*. Willy-nilly! From pillar to post. From hand to hand. Whether greasy or grasping. *Indiscriminately*!

Man   I turned up alone to meet you. I reiterate: a total stranger. A/ You could have been *anybody*: a moron or a maniac, a pervert, a poof or a paedophile, a butcher, a baker, a candlestick maker, a Marxist, a Leninist, a Zen Buddhist, a virgin or a gypsy, a legend in your own lifetime, a member of the lower orders, a nobody. (For all I knew.)

Woman   I've tried *so hard* to meet the right person. I've followed up all the avenues without success. There's no one. *This* was my last chance. (*Bursts into tears*.) Now that it hasn't worked out I think I'll/ (*Stops abruptly*.) But less about *me*. (*Eager*.) What risks did *you* take?

Man   I don't know if I should tell you.

Woman   No, do. I can take it.

Man   You can?

Woman   Yes. I can.

Man   I caught the number 38 bus.

Woman   Pardon?

Man   I could have been scarred for life.

Woman   I know.

Man   It has a reputation. The number 38 bus.

Woman   I've heard of it. Thank you for taking that risk. To be with me here tonight.

Man   That's all right. It could yet be worth it. Ha ha.

Woman   Ha ha.

Man   Ha ha.

Woman   What other risks did you take?

Man   I could have been wrong about your photograph. You could easily have turned out to have no personality.

Woman   I could. So easily. That would have been disastrous for you.

Man   No conversation.

Woman   Or catastrophic.

Man   You could have refused to pay for my beer.

Woman   Or/ You know, you really are *very* amusing.

Man   You could have refused to take me back to your place.

Woman   And wonderfully witty with it!

Man   You could have walked out and left me standing.

Woman   Yes, you really are quite a/ Oh, I could *never* have done that. I could *certainly never* have/ I love you.

Man   You/

Woman   I didn't say that. I mean: I never say things like that. I mean: I don't know what would have come over me to say such a thing as that. I/

Man   *You* don't need to worry saying things like that to *me. I* say things like that *all the time*.

Woman   I/ You do? Things like: 'I . . . love . . . you'.

Man   Well, not exactly that . . . kind of thing. But things *like* that kind of thing. Ha ha.

Woman   Ha ha. *Exactly what* kind of things?

Man   I'd be more likely to say things like – I find you *very sexually attractive*.

Woman   Oh, do you? Ha ha. Oh. I mean: do you *really* say things like that? I mean: what else do you say?

Man   I say things like: 'You're my kind of woman. And I want to sleep with you. Soon. Tonight. Now.'

Woman   You certainly say some amazing things. Ho ho.

Man   Ho ho. I also say things like: 'Where do you live? And is there anybody else there?'

Woman   You are a wonder. And strange. In many, many ways.

Man   I say things like: 'What do you like doing in bed?'

Woman   You go so far as that, do you?

Man   I do. And then I say things like: 'Fuck it. Why wait? Why don't I just place you up against a nearby wall? Why don't I rip off your black lace panties? Why don't I take out my throbbing cock and heave it up your swelling burning eagerly waiting fanny? Why don't I fill you like you've never been filled before?' And then I say things like: 'Sorry. I really will have to go.'

Woman   Is that right?

Man   That's right.

Woman   Would you be interested to know what kind of things *I* say?

Man   Fascinated.

Woman   I say things like: 'Thank you. But you must be out of your tiny fuckin' mind.' Ha ha.

Man   Ha ha.

Woman   I say things like: 'You must be the ugliest dummest arseholing creep I've ever met.' Ho ho.

Man   Ho ho.

Woman   I say things like: 'I hate you all. You are nothing but a bunch of cocksuckers. You're pricks to a man. You're cunts. You're/

Man   And do you know what I say *then*?

Woman   You're/ Please tell me.

Man   I say things like: 'Good bye. It's been nice knowing you.' Then I do things like get up and leave. Ha ha.

Woman   Ha ha.

He gets up.

Woman   Then I say things like: 'Give me back my photograph.'

Man   I say: 'You've got to be joking.' (*He puts the photograph away provocatively.*) 'I'm taking it home to shit on it.'

Woman   I say things like: 'As long as you promise.'

Man   I say things like: 'And then I'll burn it. Good bye.'

He exits.

Woman   Good bye.

Waiter *comes in.*

Waiter   Would you like anything else?

Woman   No. Thank you.

She goes into purse. Takes out money. Goes to give him it. Refrains.

Do you know I've just been stood up? Then I had this conversation with a total stranger. During it I learnt something very interesting about myself: *what a jolly nice person I am.*

He smiles. She hands over money. He takes it. She gets up and goes out.

Waiter *clears table and exits.*

The Reading Room

Characters

Man
Woman
Librarian
Supervisor

Setting

Library.

Librarian *found on behind desk. Should be marked in some way to clarify function. Tables and chairs on either side of desk.*

Man *comes in.* **Librarian** *looks up.* **Man** *smiles at* **Librarian**. *No response.* **Librarian** *goes back to work.* **Man** *sits at one table. Looks round.*

Woman *comes in, with bag.* **Man** *smiles at* **Woman**. *No response.* **Woman** *sits at other table. Takes out books, starts work.*

Man   No one ever returns your smile in the library these days. Have you found that?

Woman   I have. (*Pause.*)

Man   Are you a student?

Woman   I am. (*Pause.*)

Man   There are *many* things people don't do in the library these days. Have you found that too?

Woman   I have. Yes. (*Pause.*)

Woman *looks at* **Librarian**. **Librarian** *looks at* **Woman**. **Woman** *looks back at work.* **Librarian** *goes back to work.*

Man   And the librarian these days: if you tried to do anything she'd prevent you. Wouldn't she?

Woman   She would.

Man   I don't understand the attitude of the modern librarian. (*Pause.*) I know you.

Woman   I don't think so. (*Pause.*)

Man   I remember you from the old days.

Woman   I doubt it. (*Pause.*)

Man   You've changed.

Woman   I have not changed *one iota*!

Librarian   Quiet please.

Man   See what I mean? (*Pause.*) You *have* changed. You've changed *for the better*.

Woman   I'm glad you think so. (*Pause.*)

Man   You're a delight to behold. (*Pause.*) What are you *studying* these days?

Woman   The sexuality of the stick insect.

Man   *That's* why you're looking well. We look well when we enjoy what we do. You didn't look well when you were studying applied geomorphology.

Woman   I've never studied applied geomorphology.

Man   You *told* me you did.

Woman (*loud*)   I've *never* met you before.

Librarian *looks up.* **Man** *and* **Woman** *both look away.*
Librarian *goes back to work.*

Woman   If you'll excuse me. I *must* work. (*Pause.*)

Man   You did tell me.

Woman   You're mistaken. (*Pause.*)

Man   You used to *come round to my place* and tell me.

Woman   I don't even know where you live.

Man   Your geomorphology books under one arm. A bottle of wine under the other. You used to come right up my garden path and tell me: 'I'm studying applied geomorphology.'

Woman   I did not.

Man   Week in, week out you'd tell me: 'applied geomorphology'. Week in, week out *I'd* tell *you*: 'Give it up, it's doing nothing for your appearance.' And now you have. Thank God.

Woman   You're making this up.

Man   You suffer from a short memory.

Woman   That's just not true. I/

Man   That's why you didn't like applied geomorphology.

Woman   *What?*

Man   You could never remember it.

Woman   I can account for every episode in my life. I'm sorry: you're *just not one of them.*

Man   I've changed a lot too. Since your applied geomorphology days. I used to be blond and fat.

Woman   I've never befriended a blond person, or a fat person, let alone a blond *and* fat person. I've never gone up their garden path with a bottle of wine. Nor have I studied applied geomorphology. I'm a student of the sexuality of the stick insect. And I demand to be left alone.

Librarian   You may go outside if you wish to talk.

Man *and* **Woman** *look away.* **Woman** *goes back to work.*

Man   No. Librarians are definitely not what they used to be.

Woman   Please be quiet.

Man   I remember they used to stay off your back. They used to pretend not to hear. They used to *join in*. Didn't they?

Woman   I may have to leave. I may have to go elsewhere.

Man   And as for you:/

Woman   As for *me*?

Man   You may look better, but you *behave* worse.

Woman   I don't.

Man   You used to talk.

Woman   I did not.

Man   You used to *laugh*.

Woman   I most certainly did not.

Man   You used to ask: 'May I hold your hand?'

Woman *slaps his face.*

Librarian   I'm sorry. I will now *have to* see my supervisor.

Librarian *exits.*

Woman   That's it. I'm going. I/

Woman *starts to put her things in bag.*

Man   You used to say: 'Dammit, I'm *holding your hand.*'

She moves towards exit.

'I'm kissing you.'

She speeds up.

'I'm undoing your flies.'

She speeds up and nears exit.

'I'm putting my hand in your underpants.'

She stops.

You were so *poetic.*

She turns and lets her hair down. (Or equivalent.)

Woman   Was I? (You know what my memory's like.) Was I poetic?

Man   You were *grandiloquent.* You used to say: 'You're swelling.'

Woman   That's right.

Man   'I'm holding you.'

Woman   I did. Ha ha.

Man   'You're bulging.'

Woman   I remember it well.

Man   'I'm providing you with friction.'

Woman   I did. Didn't I?

Man   You could say it all again.

Woman   Will you be quiet afterwards?

Man   Trust me. I'll be *silent* afterwards.

Woman *comes back to table and sits. Takes out her work and appears to attend to it.*

Woman   I'm holding your hand.

Man   Gently at first.

Woman   I'm touching you.

Man   Patience.

Woman   I'm kissing you.

Man   Be less rough.

Woman   I'm undoing your flies.

Man   It's got caught.

Woman   I'm slipping my hand inside.

Man   That's better.

Woman   Inside your underpants.

Man   Lovely.

Woman   You're swelling.

Man   I'm coming along nicely.

Woman   You're bulging.

Man   I am. You're right. I am. I/

Woman   I'm providing you with friction.

Man   And you're *so* good at it. You're so/

Woman   And with my *other* hand, I/

Man   You're so/ Your *other* hand.

Woman   My *other* hand.

Man   You *don't use* your other hand.

Woman   Oh but I do. I'm loosening your belt with it.

Man   You're not.

Woman   I am. I am. I'm undoing your clip.

Man   No, don't. Do it back up.

Woman   I will not.

Man   Do it back up this minute.

Woman   Do you want me to stop?

Man   No. Oh no. Please don't stop. Just do what you used to do.

Woman   I think I'll just stop.

Man   No, please. Please.

Woman   I've stopped.

Man   Oh, please start again.

Woman   Can I do what I like?

Man   I/

Woman   Can I?

Man   Yes, all right. Yes, you can do what you like. As long as you don't/

Woman   I'm undoing your clip.

Man   Oh, oh, oh.

Woman   I'm pulling down your trousers.

Man   Ah, ah, ah.

Woman   I'm ripping off your underpants.

Man   Oh my God. You can't do that. You can't go that far. I'll be/

Woman   I'm tearing off your shirt.

Man   I'll be naked. I am naked. Oh no.

Woman   I'm wrapping my lips round your/

Man   You're disgusting. You/ (*He gets up.*) I just don't know what's got into you since the old days. You never used to strip me, in the old days. I mean; look at me. I'm naked. Ha ha. I have no clothes on. Ho ho. How embarrassing for me. This is a library. This is a reading room. This is a public place. Hee hee.

Librarian *and* **Supervisor** *come in, unseen by him.* **Woman** *goes back to work.*

Man   Oh, stop it, please. Stop it, please, somebody. I/ (*Turns and sees* **Librarian** *and* **Supervisor**.) Oh, hello there. Hello. Ha ha. Ha ha. Ha? It was all just a laugh. Just a joke. (*Turns to* **Woman**.) Wasn't it. Tell them it was just a joke. Tell them.

Woman *goes back to work.*

Man (*to* **Librarian** *and* **Supervisor**)   In the old days she only used one hand.

He exits.

Waiting for Shuggie's Ma

Characters

Gus, *sixteen years old*
Stu, *sixteen years old*

Setting

A verandah on the top floor of a block of flats. There is a clothes line with sheets, which are all but concealing the glass door and windows at the back of the verandah.

Waiting for Shuggie's Ma may look long on the page. In fact, it should run to no longer than twelve minutes.

Gus *and* **Stu** *are found on stage, standing at the front of the verandah.*

Gus   It's good up here but.

Stu   Aye. (No bad.)

Gus   It's brilliant.

Stu   *Oh* aye. (Aye.)

Pause.

Gus   Thirty-five floors and all.

Stu   Aye. (No.)

Gus   Thirty-five floors to the top of the building. (What?)

Stu   Is it fuck.

Gus   What?

Stu   Is it fuck thirty-five floors to the top of the building.

Gus   No?

Stu   No!

Gus   Aw.

Pause.

Stu   Thirty-*four* floors.

Gus   Eh?

Stu   Thirty-*four* floors to the top of the building.

Gus   Aye?

Stu   Aye!

Gus   Aw.

Pause.

At least you see dead far.

Stu   Aye.

Gus   At least you see dead far from the top of the building.

Stu   You see right across Glasgow from the top of the building.

Gus   You see to Manchester from the top of the building.

Stu   You see to/ Can you fuck.

Gus   You see to/ (What?)

Stu   Can you fuck see to Manchester from the top of the building.

Gus   No?

Stu   No.

Gus   Aw.

Pause.

Well we can see the Boys' Brigade from the top of the building.

Stu   Aye.

Gus   The Boys' Brigade Hall.

Stu   Aye. (Definitely, man.)

Gus   Aye?

Stu   Aye!

Gus   Aw.

Pause.

And the Boys' Brigade get out in a minute.

Stu   Aye. (*Oh* aye.)

Gus   Aye. Out for their wee break.

Stu   Aye. Out for their fly-smoke.

Gus   Aye. Out for a scratch of their balls.

Stu   Aye. Out for a sly slash up against a wall.

Gus   Aye. Out for a quick wank.

Stu   Aye. (No!)

Gus   (Ha-ha.)

Stu   *Oh* no: quick wank nothing!

Gus   Aye quick wank ha ha but!

Stu   Quick wank ha ha?

Gus   Aye, because/

Stu   Oh *aye*. Ha ha *definitely*.

Gus   Because the Boys' Brigade are a *right* toss-off squad.

Stu   Aye.

Gus   Aye?

Stu   Aye!

Gus   Aw.

Pause.

Gus   So the Boys' Brigade wanks are due out.

Stu   Aye.

Gus   And. The Boys' Brigade wanks will look about.

Stu   *Oh* aye. (Definitely.)

Gus   Look up and see *us*.

Stu   No.

Gus   Look up and see *me*.

Stu   No!

Gus   And I'll flash my arse.

Stu   No. (*Oh* no.)

Gus   No?

Stu   No!

Gus   Aw.

Pause.

Stu   Because when the Boys' Brigade wanks look up, they won't see you.

Gus   Aw.

Stu   They won't see me.

Gus   Aw.

Stu   They'll see two dots at the top of the building.

Gus   Aw.

Pause.

Two dots at the top of the building?

Stu   Aye.

Gus   Aw.

Pause.

It is good up here but, *isn't it*?

Stu   Aye. (No bad.)

Gus   I mean. See Shuggie's ma's sheets, right?

Stu   These sheets here?

Gus   Aye. These sheets here. Brilliant, aren't they?

Stu   No.

Gus   Brilliant sheets! (What?)

Stu   No.

Gus   No?

Stu   No!

Gus   Aw.

Pause.

Stu   Wank sheets.

Gus   Aw.

Stu   Bastard sheets.

Gus   Aw.

Stu   Fucking Boys' Brigade headbanger sheets.

Gus   Aw.

Pause.

It's good up here but.

Stu   Aye. (No bad.)

Gus   It's good up here waiting for Shuggie's ma.

Stu   Aye, *no*! (Is it fuck.)

Gus   No?

Stu   No!

Gus   Aw.

Stu   It's bastarding boring waiting for Shuggie's ma.

Gus   Aw.

Stu   So Shuggie's ma bastarding better hurry up.

Gus   Aw.

Pause.

At least the top of the building shakes.

Stu   Aye.

Gus   Shakes in the wind.

Stu   *Oh* aye. It shakes like a zombie.

Gus   Aye. It shakes like a bastard.

Stu   Aye. It shakes like a dick.

Gus   Aye. It shakes like a bastarding zombie.

Stu   Aye. It shakes like a bastarding zombie's dick.

Gus   Aye. It shakes like/

Pause.

Like a bastarding zombie's dick?

Stu   Aye.

Gus   Aw.

Pause.

And Shuggie's ma's hoose is brilliant.

Stu   Aye, *no*! And is it fuck.

Gus   Is it fuck?

Stu   Aye, is it fuck.

Gus   Aw.

Stu   It's a pure dive.

Gus   Aw.

Pause.

Stu   So who gived you the keys?

Gus   Eh? (So I met Shuggie.)

Stu   Who gived you the keys to Shuggie's ma's hoose?

Gus   I met Shuggie and he gave me the keys to his ma's hoose. Aye, I met the cunt, I got him to come across with the keys. I met the bastard, the bastard's on his way to the Boys' Brigade. I met him, I threatened to bop the bampot one on the nut, he doesn't come across with the keys to his ma's hoose. He says: 'I'll give you the keys to my ma's house if you promise not to mark my ma's good furniture.' So I says: 'I'll mark you, you don't come across with the keys. You don't walk across with the keys. Shuggie boy, I'll walk across you.'

Stu   Aye and you know *what*, Gus?

Gus   *What*, Stu?

Stu   You mark Shuggie's ma's good furniture, *Shuggie's ma* will mark you.

Gus   Shuggie's ma?

Stu   Aye, Shuggie's ma.

Gus   Aw.

Pause.

Stu   Because Shuggie's ma is a big bird.

Gus   Aw.

Pause.

So how will we know when Shuggie's ma's back?

Stu   What?

Gus   We're out on Shuggie's ma's verandah, so how will we know when Shuggie's ma's back in her hoose?

Stu   We'll see her.

Gus   How will we know she's back from the bingo?

Stu   We'll see Shuggie's ma coming in at the bottom of the building.

Gus   Aw.

Pause.

No! We will not see Shuggie's ma at the bottom of the building.

Stu   How come?

Gus   Because Shuggie's ma will be a dot at the bottom of the building.

Stu   So?

Gus   So we won't know which dot at the bottom of the building Shuggie's ma *is*.

Stu   Aye.

Gus   No.

Stu   Aye we *will*.

Gus   How come?

Stu   Because Shuggie's ma will be a red dot at the bottom of the building.

Gus   Aw.

Stu   Because Shuggie's ma wears a red coat.

Gus   Aw.

They look down. Pause.

Stu   The only trouble is, Gus:/

Gus   What's that, Stu?

Stu   It's also bastarding boring looking down at the bottom of the building.

Gus   Bastarding boring?

Stu   Aye.

Gus   Aw.

Pause.

So, Stu.

Stu   What, Gus?

Gus   Do you remember I gave a Boys' Brigade wank a tanking?

Stu   The time you . . . you . . . /

Gus   A tanking outside the Boys' Brigade Hall.

Stu   Aye? Aye, *oh* aye. (*Definitely* some tanking you gave the wank.)

Gus   So he says to me, he says: 'So, cunt, you are the only cunt *here* is not in the Boys' Brigade, cunt.'

Stu   Aye. Oh aye, Gus. Because then you says, you says:

'Too fucking right, cunt. And that's why you've had it. Aye, you, cunt, are going to get bopped.'

Gus   I did.

Stu   Brilliant, man.

Gus   Was I?

Stu   Aye.

Gus   Was I brilliant?

Stu   *Oh* aye.

Gus   Aw.

Pause.

So ho. So: the wank swung a couple of miss-hit bops at us. (Soft cunt.)

Stu   So you kneed him one to the balls.

Gus   Aye. I bopped him one to the belly.

Stu   Aye. You butted him one on the nut.

Gus   Aye. And I pinned him on the ground.

Stu   Aye. And you/

Gus   And I/

Stu   And you/

Gus   And I practically farted in his fucking face. Ha ha. Aye. (The cunt.)

Pause.

So it was a *clear fucking victory*.

Stu   *Oh* aye.

Gus   But did you hear what the cheeky cunt says to us but?

Stu   (Definitely.)

Gus   He says: 'Do you give in?'

Stu   *Oh* aye.

Gus   'Do you give in.'

Stu   *Oh* aye.

Gus   The mental fucking headbanger Boys' Brigade wank merchant . . . And it was a clear fucking victory too. A clear fucking victory, so he shoots up the road to fuck, bleeding to bastardy. (The cunt.)

Stu   Aye.

Gus   Aye, and he shoots up the road *right into* Shuggie's ma.

Stu   Aye, right into Shuggie's ma.

Gus   Shuggie's fucking ma.

Stu   Shuggie's ma who takes the cunt/

Gus   Fucking *takes* the cunt.

Stu   The cunt who/ (This bit's brilliant.)

Gus   This is the best bit.

Stu   The Boys' Brigade wank merchant!

Gus   So she takes the Boys' Brigade wank merchant up to her hoose here.

Stu   Aye.

Gus   Up to her hoose here and the Boys' Brigade wank merchant does not get to emerge, does not get to get *out*, for a full *two hours* later.

Stu   *Oh* no.

Gus   No.

Stu   That *was* the best bit.

Gus   That bit *was* brilliant.

Stu   *Oh* aye.

Gus   Aye. Aye?

Stu   Aye.

Gus   Aw.

Pause.

Stu   So me first to meet Shuggie's ma.

Gus   What? No!

Stu   Aye.

Gus   Aye?

Stu   Aye.

Gus   Aw.

Pause.

How come you first to meet Shuggie's ma?

Stu   How come?

Gus   How come!

Stu   Me first to meet Shuggie's ma – Shuggie's ma is a big, experienced bird – because it was *my idea* to meet Shuggie's ma, *at all.*

Gus   Your idea?

Stu   Aye.

Gus   Aw.

Pause.

So? . . . *So* if it was your idea to meet Shuggie's ma?

Stu   Me first.

Gus   *So* if it was your idea?

Stu   Me first.

Gus   Because I got the key off Shuggie.

Stu   Me first. (Because it was my idea.)

Gus   *I* got the key off Shuggie, for Shuggie's ma's hoose.

Stu   It was my idea and shut the cakehole.

Gus   Your idea?

Stu   My idea.

Gus   Aw . . . Shut the cakehole?

Stu   Shut the cakehole.

Gus   Aw.

Pause.

Stu   So *me* first to meet Shuggie's ma.

Gus   You first?

Stu   Because Shuggie's ma is a big, experienced bird.

Gus   Aw.

Stu   And because it *doesn't fucking matter* who goes first.

Gus   Aw.

Pause.

So what'll Shuggie's ma say to you?

Stu   What?

Gus   What'll Shuggie's ma say to you when you walk into Shuggie's ma's living room?

Stu   What'll Shuggie's ma say to me?

Gus   What'll Shuggie's ma say to you?

Stu   What'll Shuggie's ma *do* to me?

Gus   Eh? I don't know.

Stu   Aye. What'll Shuggie's ma do to *my body*?

Gus   I don't know.

Stu   And what'll Shuggie's ma *make me* do to *her* body?

Gus   I don't know.

Stu   Because *whatever* she makes me do, I'll *do* it.

Gus   Aw.

Pause.

Stu   And heh, Gus.

Gus   What, Stu?

Stu   Remember to keep looking for Shuggie's ma.

Gus   Shuggie's ma – the red dot at the bottom of the building?

Stu   Aye.

Gus   Aw.

Stu   Aye.

Gus   OK.

They look out.

So, Stu.

Stu   What, Gus?

Gus   So there's the/

Stu   What?

Gus   There's the/

Stu   Where?

Gus   There's the Boys' Brigade out for their wee break. (Eh?)

Stu   Out for their fly smoke.

Gus   All the black dots outside the Boys' Brigade Hall.

Stu   *Oh* aye.

Gus   Aye. (Out for their sly slash.)

Stu   Aye, well/

Gus   Aye. Out for their quick wank.

Stu   Aye, well/

Gus   Quick wank, ha ha but!

Stu   Aye, well, just keep looking for Shuggie's ma. (Ha ha, fuck off.)

Gus   Ha ha, fuck off?

Stu   Ha ha, fuck off!

Gus   Aw.

Long pause.

So, Stu.

Stu   What, Gus?

Gus   Let's *show* these Boys' Brigade wanks.

Stu   No, we/

Gus   Because/

Stu   No/

Gus   Because/

Stu   They'll look up and see a couple of dots at the top of the building.

Gus   *Eh?*

Stu   Two dots in front of Shuggie's ma's sheets.

Gus   Shuggie's ma's sheets?

Stu   Aye.

Gus   Shuggie's ma's *sheets?*

Stu   *Oh* aye.

Gus   Aw.

Pause. He yanks a sheet off the line and starts waving it over the verandah.

Stu   What is this?

Gus   Haw, you Boys' Brigade wanks.

Stu   What *the fuck* is this?

Gus   You Boys' Brigade tools.

Stu *takes the other sheet off the line.*

Gus   You cunts. You wanks. Look at me.

Stu *starts waving.*

Stu   Look at *us*.

Gus   Aye, look at us.

Stu   You tools.

Gus   You headbangers.

Stu   You *Boys' Brigade* headbangers.

Gus/Stu   Fuck bastarding off.

Pause. They stop waving.

Gus   Think the Boys' Brigade wanks saw us waving at them, Stu?

Stu   I don't know, Gus . . . Because they are nothing but a bunch of black dots outside the Boys' Brigade Hall.

Gus   Aw.

Pause.

Heh, Stu.

Stu   What, Gus?

Gus   But what if they see the two dots *climbing down* Shuggie's ma's sheets?

Stu   Eh?

Gus   Climbing down Shuggie's ma's verandah to the verandah below?

Stu No.

Gus No?

Stu *Oh* no.

Gus Aw.

Pause.

Stu Because: they'll look up and see/

Gus They'll look up and see/

Stu They'll see/

Gus/Stu *Two dots* climbing down Shuggie's ma's sheets.

Pause.

Stu So they won't know who/

Gus Heh, Stu.

Stu They won't know who the two dots are. (What, Gus?)

Gus They will know who the two dots are, because Shuggie'll tell them.

Pause.

Stu I'm not climbing down no building.

Gus No?

Stu No. (I'm meeting Shuggie's ma.)

Gus Aw.

Stu And if I *did* climb down the building, I'd be fucked if I'd climb back up it.

Gus Aw.

Pause.

Stu Besides the black dots have fucked off.

Gus Fucked off?

Stu Aye.

Gus   Oh *no*.

Stu   Aye. Fucked off from outside the Boys' Brigade Hall.

Gus   Aw.

Pause.

The Boys' Brigade must've gone back in.

Stu   Aye.

Gus   After their 'wee break'.

Stu   *Oh* aye.

Gus   So you don't think the Boys' Brigade wanks saw us, Stu? (Surely to fuck.)

Stu   I don't know.

Gus   They must've seen us waving Shuggie's ma's sheets!

Stu   I don't know.

Gus   Because/

Stu   Ssshhh . . . (I heard a cunt.)

Pause.

Gus   What cunt was that?

Stu   Shhh . . . I'm sure I heard a cunt *walking about*.

Pause.

Gus   Heh. Cunt. Who the fuck are you?

Stu   Ssshhh . . . (It must be Shuggie's ma.)

Gus   Shuggie's *ma*?

Stu   Aye.

Gus   Aw.

Pause.

Oh no.

Stu   Oh *yes*. *Definitely* Shuggie's ma.

Gus *looks about.*

Gus   Heh, Stu.

Stu   Heh, Gus.

Gus   We forgot to keep on looking down.

Stu   I wonder what Shuggie's ma will do to me.

Gus   *I* forgot to keep on looking down.

Stu   What Shuggie's ma will do *to my body*.

Gus   Down at the bottom of the building.

Stu   Or what she'll make *me* do to *her* body.

Gus   Because it was bastarding boring looking down. (Stu.)

Pause.

Sorry.

Stu   It's all right.

Gus   Is it all right?

Stu   Aye.

Gus   Aw.

Pause.

Gus   And heh, Stu.

Stu   What, Gus?

Gus   What's all those black dots at the bottom of the building? . . . Those black dots *coming in* the building?

They look down together and at each other.

Stu/Gus   It's the Boys' Brigade!

Pause.

Gus   So fucking brilliant!

Stu   The shower of wanks.

Gus   So they must've seen us waving Shuggie's ma's sheets.

Stu   The headbangers.

Gus   Fucking ace.

Stu   The headbanging Boys' Brigade bampots.

Gus   The Boys' Brigade are coming to get us.

Stu   Because I only wanted to meet Shguggie's ma.

Pause.

Gus   So, Stu.

Stu   What, Gus?

Gus   Come, we'll climb down Shuggie's ma's sheets *now*?

Stu   No.

Gus   And make 'the getaway'.

Stu   *Oh* no.

Gus   No?

Stu   No.

Gus   Aw.

The Education of a Gentle Pervert

Characters

Older Man
Younger Man

Setting

Bench

Older Man *walks on, wearing sunglasses, carrying bag. He stops, sits, puts bag down, takes out apple, takes out knife, cuts apple, eats, puts down knife and apple. Takes out magazine, holding it closed, looks round, opens it gingerly. It has pictures of nude boys on the back and front and it is called* Just Boys. *Just as he settles to read, he hears a noise and quickly folds and conceals his magazine.* **Younger Man** *walks on, wearing sunglasses and carrying bag. He crosses in front of* **Older Man**, *stops, looks round unostentatiously, pauses and exits.* **Older Man** *watches him go, over his glasses, catches himself, stops. Settles again to read magazine.* **Younger Man** *re-enters.* **Older Man** *conceals magazine again abruptly.* **Younger Man** *crosses in front of* **Older Man**, *stops, looks round, crosses back* diagonally *in front of* **Older Man**, *stops, tries the ground and is satisfied. He takes a towel from his bag, lays it out, lies down on his front and settles.* **Older Man** *observes him carefully and tries to put his magazine into his bag, unobserved. As he is about to put it into his bag,* **Younger Man** *sits up.* **Older Man** *holds his magazine to one side.* **Younger Man** *sits up.* **Older Man** *folds and holds his magazine to one side.* **Younger Man** *goes into his bag.* **Older Man** *sees this and when* **Younger Man** *turns towards him he looks away quickly.* **Younger Man** *studies* **Older Man** *carefully before taking out and opening his magazine. It has nude pictures of older men in it and it is called* Mature Beauty. **Younger Man** *settles reading it, lying on his back.* **Older Man** *gradually turns his attention back to* **Younger Man** *and is palpably stunned by what he sees. So stunned that he looks away again, smiles bashfully at his own magazine and to and fro between his and* **Younger Man**'s *magazine before settling his gaze on* **Younger Man**. **Younger Man** *peeks out from under his magazine and looks directly at* **Older Man**. *As soon as* **Older Man** *realises he is sharing a look, he looks away abruptly, stands and exits, stuffing his magazine into his bag as he goes.* **Younger Man** *watches him leave, before settling back down with magazine.* **Older Man** *re-enters unnoticed, sits, taking magazine back out and holding it ostentatiously towards* **Younger Man**. **Older Man** *peeks out above his magazine, deliberately making a sound.* **Younger Man** *quickly tries to conceal his magazine, the noise impact from which makes* **Older Man** *do likewise and look away.* **Younger Man** *turns and is surprised to see return of* **Older Man** *and studies him carefully.* **Younger Man** *puts magazine down and takes off his top, lying down on his front.* **Older Man** *looks at* **Younger Man** *and, startled,* *looks away again.* **Younger Man** *picks up his magazine and turns, pointing it towards* **Older Man**. **Older Man** *turns slowly towards* **Younger Man**, *his face concealed by the magazine. Slowly he peeks out and enjoys studying* **Younger Man**'s *body.* **Younger Man** *peeks out and* **Older Man** *retreats behind magazine.* **Younger Man** *sees this, puts magazine down and stands. He removes shoes and moves to one side of* **Older Man** *and turns his back. Very slowly he starts to undo his trousers and slip them down. As he does so,* **Older Man** *peeks out again and is transfixed. Suddenly* **Younger Man** *yanks up his trousers and* **Older Man** *looks away abruptly.*

Younger man *lies down on his front.* **Older man** *looks out, studies* **Younger Man**, *puts magazine down, goes to remove his top, catches sight of his body, looks to and fro comparatively between his and* **Younger Man**'s *body, replaces top. Stares further at* **Younger Man**, *looks round, gingerly slips hand into pocket. With almost imperceptible slowness, he starts to masturbate. Just begins to become perceptible when* **Younger Man** *turns towards him and smiles.* **Older Man** *freezes, not looking away from* **Younger Man** *until he very slowly takes hand from pocket, acting nonchalant.* **Younger Man** *turns away again.* **Older Man** *looks away and back slowly. Looks at* **Younger Man**'s *body, steels himself, gets up and, stretching out his hand, moves towards* **Younger Man**. **Younger Man** *turns back and* **Older Man** *realigns his course and exits abruptly.* **Younger Man** *watches him go, looks round, sees bag, crosses to it and picks it up, holds it up and goes to shout after* **Older Man**. *Thinks better of it. Puts it down. Lays down again on his front.* **Older Man** *re-enters, gingerly.* **Younger man** *stirs.* **Older Man** *halts.* **Younger Man** *settles.* **Older Man** *continues, picks up bag and goes to go.* **Younger Man** *turns to see this.* **Older Man** *stops.* **Younger Man** *turns back.* **Older Man** *goes into his bag and brings out a camera, puts bag down, looks through camera and focuses it on* **Younger Man**. **Younger Man** *turns towards* **Older Man**, *who looks away abruptly as if taking a photograph of the grass.* **Younger Man** *observes this. Suddenly* **Younger Man** *stands, and takes off his trousers to reveal sporty boxer shorts. Lies down again on his front.* **Older Man** *slowly turns camera towards* **Younger Man**. *Stunned by what he sees he abruptly lowers the camera. Looks to and fro between camera and* **Younger Man** *and expresses self-disgust. Turns away, puts camera in bag. As he does so,* **Younger Man** *turns on to his back, looks* *thoughtfully at* **Older Man**, *puts hand inside boxer shorts and starts to masturbate.* **Older Man** *goes to go.* **Younger Man** *sees this, coughs and continues masturbating nonchalantly.* **Older Man** *turns back, sees* **Younger Man** *masturbating, turns away, looks round, returns to bench, sits, puts bag down, puts hand in pocket and starts to masturbate. Slowly turns to* **Younger Man** *who then promptly turns on his front.* **Older Man** *stops masturbating and looks away. Looks back slowly, thinks for a second and resumes masturbating, gets frantic, stands up, inching towards* **Younger Man**, *still masturbating. As he gets close to* **Younger Man**, **Younger Man** *turns abruptly on his back.* **Older Man** *changes course, steps over* **Younger Man** *and walks off.* **Younger Man** *watches him go and slaps the ground, in disappointment and resignation. He dresses and goes to go. Passes bench, stops, looks at* **Older Man**'s *bag, looks round and goes into bag. Pulls out knife, goes to put it back, sees* **Older Man** *coming, concentrates on continuing to search, brings out camera, throws knife away and leaps back to his face-down lying position, concealing camera.* **Older Man** *enters, goes to bag, picks it up, goes to go, turns to see* **Younger Man**, *startled to see he is now dressed, shrugs and goes to walk off.* **Younger Man** *turns and sits up.*

Younger Man   Come back.

Older Man *stops. Pauses. Continues.*

Younger Man (*with menace*)   I said: *come back.*

Older Man *stops. Pause. Continues.* **Younger Man** *goes after him and blocks his way.*

Younger Man   Didn't you hear me?

Older Man   I/

Older Man *turns to go other way.*

Younger Man   Your behaviour is very hurtful.

Older Man   You/ Pardon me?

Younger Man   I thought you were trying to hurt my feelings.

Older Man   Oh no. No. not at all. Why, I/

Younger Man   So why don't you take your clothes off?

Older Man   I/ Excuse me?

Younger Man   You could undress, if you like.

Older Man   Here?

Younger Man   Here.

Older Man   Now.

Younger Man   Now. (*Pause.*)

Older Man   Oh ho ho ho ho. I couldn't.

Younger Man   *I* did.

Older Man   I/ You did. It's true. You/

Younger Man   So why don't *you*?

Older Man   I/ No. (Thank you. I/) I mean: I/

Younger Man   Why not?

Older Man   I don't have your/ I'm not so/ I'm *shy*.

Younger Man   I find you very attractive.

Older Man   I/ Oh, ho ho *ho*. You don't. (*Do you?*)

Younger Man   I do . . . Please.

Older Man   I/

Younger Man   Please take your clothes off.

Older Man *looks round, takes off his top, shows himself to* **Younger Man**.

Younger Man   Lovely.

Older Man   Oh/ I/ Do you really think so?

Younger Man   I do. I do *indeed* . . . And the trousers?

Older Man   I/ The trousers.

Younger Man   Yes, the trousers. *And* the socks.

Older Man   I/ Oh/ Ha ha. The socks?

Younger Man   Yes. The socks.

Older Man   Right: the socks. The/ Why?

Younger Man   *Why*?

Older Man   I/ Yes. I mean: what would you like me to do when I/

Younger Man   I would like to explore your body.

Older Man   I/ What?

Younger Man   Access!

Older Man   You/ ? *Access?*

Younger Man   Yes, access to the exploration of your body.

Older Man   I/

Younger Man   (You know.)

Older Man   I do.

Younger Man   Whenever the fancy take me.

Older Man   Oh, *very* good. I/

Younger Man   So if you'll just/

Older Man   Certainly. I/ I mean: right away. Ha ha.

He takes off his socks and trousers and raises his arms.

Well.

Younger Man   Well?

Older Man   This is me.

Younger Man   It certainly is.

Older Man   And I'm all yours.

Younger Man   Good. Ha. ha.

Older Man   As they say. Ha ha.

Younger Man   Ha ha. As they say.

Older Man   I/

He moves towards **Younger Man**. **Younger Man** *dodges him.*

Is there anything the matter? I/

Younger Man   You've forgotten your glasses.

Older Man   I/ Oh *yes*. Of *course*. My *glasses*. You're *so* right. My/

He takes off glasses and puts them in bag.

How silly of me. Now:/

He moves towards **Younger Man**.

Younger Man   I'd like to ask you to do something for me.

Older Man   I/ You/ Of course. Whatever you/

Younger Man   Lie down.

Older Man   I/ Lie down?

Younger Man   On the bench.

Older Man   Lie down on the/ On *this* bench?

Younger Man   On this bench.

Older Man   Oh, certainly. Ha ha. I mean:/

Older Man *looks round, looks at* **Younger man**, **Younger Man** *gestures encouragement and* **Older Man** *lies on his back.*

Younger Man   Could you lie on your front?

Older Man   I/

Younger Man   Would you mind?

Older Man   Why, I/ No! I mean, I/ Ha ha.

Older Man *turns over and lies on his stomach.*

Younger Man   Thank you.

Older Man   That's ah . . . all right. I/ And what would you be thinking of/ ? I mean:/

Younger Man   I'm going to explore you.

Older Man   Oh ah?

Younger Man   I'll be giving you a thorough exploring.

Older Man   That's good.

Younger Man   Whenever it suits me.

Older Man   That's very good. Whenever it suits you?

Younger Man   It is. It does. It suits me now. So just relax.

Older Man   I'll certainly. I'll, eh/ I'll *do my best.*

Younger Man *takes out camera and looks through lens and lines it up to take a photo of* **Older Man**. *Technical hitch.*

Younger Man   Shit.

Older Man   Is there anything wrong? I mean: eh/

Younger Man   Everything's fine. Everything's/

Older Man   Good. Ah, I/ I'm very glad you're going to 'explore' me. Ha ha.

Younger Man   Ha ha.

Older Man   Ha ha.

Younger Man *fumbles frantically. Thinks he's sorted problem. Lines up photograph again. Problem still there.*

Younger Man   Fuck it. What's the matter with this/ ?

Older Man   What's the matter?

Younger Man   Nothing. I/ Just relax. Please. I/

Camera *flashes by accident.* **Younger Man** *turns away.*

Older Man   What are you doing? Why are you/ ?

Older Man *turns towards* **Younger Man**.

Younger Man   Nothing. I/ It's all right. You just lie there. You just/

Younger Man *turns with camera, prepared to take photograph, to be confronted by* **Older Man** *looking directly at him.*

Older Man   I don't/ I/ You/ What are you/ ?

Older Man *leaps off bench in terror.*

Younger Man   I told you to lie down.

Older Man   But you can't possibly/

Younger Man   I told you I was going to/ Who can't?

Older Man   You/ 'Who can't?'

Younger Man   Who can't!

Older Man   I/

Younger Man   So lie down.

Older Man   You/

Younger Man   *Lie down*!

Older Man   No.

Younger Man   Yes.

Older Man   I mean: I'm totally unable to/

Younger Man *picks up knife and points it at* **Older Man**.

Younger Man   Lie down.

Older Man   Oh no. You've got completely the wrong/ I'm just not that sort of/ I mean: how can I/ ? Here! I/ OK.

Older Man *lies down on back.*

Younger Man   On your front.

Older Man *doesn't move.* **Younger Man** *holds knife towards him.*

Older Man   I/ Yes/ All right. I/ Whatever you/

Younger Man   On your front.

Older Man *turns over.* **Younger Man** *takes photos.* **Older Man** *flinches with each flash.*

Younger Man   Now stand up.

Older Man   I/ Stand up? You/ Why?

Younger Man   Stand up.

Older Man *stands up.*

Younger Man   Hold yourself.

Older Man   Oh no. Now you're not taking my/ You're not/

Younger Man   *Hold yourself!*

Older Man   My/ Hold myself? I/ Certainly!

Older Man *wraps his arms around his shoulders and back.* **Younger Man** *holds knife towards* **Older Man**. **Older Man** *holds his penis.*

Younger Man   Good.

He takes photographs.

Thank you.

Older Man   You're welcome. Can I get dressed now?

Younger Man   By all means.

Younger Man *repacks bag. And goes to go.* **Older Man** *is still only slightly dressed.*

Older Man   Are you going?

Younger Man *stops.*

Older Man   Could I possibly have my camera back?

Younger Man *turns to face him.*

Older Man   It was rather expensive. I/

Younger Man *takes out camera.*

Older Man   Thank you.

Younger Man *removes spool and gives* **Older Man** *camera.*

Younger Man   You're welcome.

Younger Man *goes to go.*

Older Man   Have you got any plans for those photographs?

Younger Man   I'm going to explore them. At my leisure. Whenever the fancy takes me.

Older Man   I/ Oh, good. That's very/

Younger Man   I find you very attractive.

Older Man   You/

Younger Man *goes.*

Older Man   He's going to explore me. At his leisure. Me! Whenever the fancy takes him. Ha ha.

He realises he's almost naked, he picks up clothes and covers himself reflexly and goes to go. Stops, looks round.

But then he finds me . . . *very attractive.*

Older Man *goes.*